It was gonna be like Paris

It was gonna be like Paris

Emily Listfield

The Dial Press
New York

Lines from "Frenchette" by David Johansen used with permission of the author.

Lines from "The Hollow Men" by T.S. Eliot used with permission of Faber and Faber Publishers, London, England.

LIBRARY OF CONGRESS CATALOGING IN PUBLICATION DATA
Listfield, Emily.
It was gonna be like Paris.

I. Title.
PS3562.I782218   1984   813′.54
Library of Congress Catalog Card Number 83-7195
ISBN 0-385-27939-6

For My Parents

Waking alone
At the hour when we are
Trembling with tenderness
Lips that would kiss
Form prayers to broken stone.
—*T.S. Eliot*
"The Hollow Men"

You call that love in French
But it's just Frenchette
I've been to France
So let's just dance.
—*David Johansen*
"Frenchette"

It was gonna be like Paris

p. 20

*T*he hot club in New York that summer had a huge graffiti-like sign painted on one of its walls. It said: Fuck Art, Let's Dance.

I liked going there every now and then. I liked dancing for hours, even though the place was not well air-conditioned, and within five minutes, I would be as soaked as if caught in a summer storm.

I liked sweating, I liked forgetting—til about five or six in the morning. It was okay. For a little while, it was all okay.

*T*his month, every boarded-up building, every spare wall, every doorway in the neighborhood has received the same treatment. A circle with two parallel lines drawn through the upper quadrant. Horizontal lines for eyes, a mouth. Three lines sticking up outside of the circle—hair. Blind Youth, it says beneath it. On every sidestreet, on every phone booth, Blind Youth, Blind Youth, Blind Youth. There is one wall where it differs. All of the lines are outside the circle. Blind Youth Explodes, it says.

*O*f course, I knew right away that he was a trouble boy. Like all trouble boys, the ones who court destruction and pretty ladies. They're real good at dancing with both, and then walking away, before the final quakes, with the same assured swagger, the same grace, that you knew all along was danger, real danger, but you were too hooked to care. Those pied pipers have the strut down pat. Brett.

*C*arrie looks something like a cross between a bag lady and a Vogue model. Today she is wearing a white waiter's jacket with nothing underneath, rolled-up khaki shorts and uptown black patent leather sandals. And pearl earrings. She almost always wears pearl earrings. She has long legs and fair skin and she always looks, well, however it is she always looks, she always looks good and people always look. It doesn't matter what you wear, Carrie says, as long as you have the right haircut. And of course, she does.

*S*treet music.
Salsa and rumba and rap and disco and reggae and pop. Tell me what you're listening to. Tell me what you hear. You're gonna hear this. Turn up that box, man, let 'em hear this. Can you name that tune?

*H*e called to say good morning. He called to say good afternoon. He called to say goodnight. He called to say he loved my hair when it was falling out of a ponytail. He called to say he really didn't have anything to say but felt like talking to me anyway. He called to ask if I would see him the next night.

Of course, of course. How could I not?

*S*ee, it was gonna be like this. There were gonna be painters and writers and musicians and dancers and actors and we were all gonna be special and charmed and we would meet each other and inspire each other and admire each other and work together and work apart and we would help each other and we would all be interesting and interested and we would all be talented and kind and it was all gonna be special and charmed. It was gonna be like Paris in the twenties, it was gonna be like Berlin, it was gonna be all of us at once thinking and feeling we could make it right, and we were gonna, too, make it all special and charmed. That's how it was gonna be, that's how it was gonna be.

*S*he's going at it with a hacksaw, he said. She won't leave me alone. You'd think she'd get the idea by now that I don't want to let her in on everything. But the more distance I create, the more ammunition she comes armed with. She just won't leave me alone, he said.

He refuses to talk to me, she said. He says there's nothing to talk about. Then if I get upset, which I always do, it turns into a don't-get-upset conversation and we don't get anywhere. He says he likes me as much as he'll ever like anyone, but he doesn't believe in love. It's been five years. Five years ago, he believed in love, she said, I have the letters to prove it.

*T*rading up, trading down. Do you know of anything? Have you heard of anything? Anything? Anything?

Wandering about the streets at dawn, newspaper and pen in hand, clustered around phone booths, glassy-eyed, possessed. What about this one? Or this one? Already rented. Too late. Too small. Too much.

Carrie's looking too. She reads the obituaries along with the classified ads. Dead old people. Vacant apartments. A few discreet phone calls. It couldn't hurt.

Do you know of anything? Anything?

I screwed the gummy caps back onto the mangled tubes of color. We had reached an impasse, my painting and I. I had given it Athena's birth, but it had yet to inhale its first breath, to take its first steps without my overprotective hands. I sat across the room and listened for its sign language.

Torrential rain racing furiously with the wind, crashing into the pavement, railing into the windows, and two men arguing vociferously in Spanish, and the phone ringing and ringing unanswered upstairs, and the one-dimensional Chopin sputtering from the radio.

I waited for the one thing that could transcend this cacophony. I waited for the painting to begin its mime. I listened for its instructions. I watched for it to progress into order. I turned off the radio. And I waited.

The charcoal gray is overpowering the eyes. And the hands, they should be an inch lower. And that triangle of cobalt blue has got to be lightened.

I washed out my brushes and started again.

*T*here are no geniuses living in the East Village, my landlord says. If you were all so smart, he says, you would be living uptown.

*H*is lips. I should tell you about Brett's lips. His disarming, disturbing, mesmerizing lips. Lips designed solely for the nuances of romance.

The way he moved them, the way he spoke. How they seemed continually on the verge of forming a kiss, a slow, slow luxurious kiss. How subtly his mouth could tease and mock with the simplest of inflections. How gently he caressed each word as it formed. How, when not in use, those lips would rest in a smirk that even Da Vinci's brush could not hope to capture. And how infuriating was his pursed lip expression when he withdrew into his own thoughts, when he would not speak.

His lips were one of his most effective weapons, immune to logic.

*T*hat first night, I said to him, Look, I have to sleep with the sheets over my head, and he crawled under them and said, If you wanted to sleep with hay covering you, that would be okay with me.

*H*e couldn't weigh more than ninety-five pounds, and of course, he's dieting. With his blue-black hair, last year platinum, and his kohl-lined eyes, he really is quite the petite femme fatale. He was late for work the other day because he got delayed hitting a businessman in the head with a bottle.

It seems this three piece suit number hit his dog with an attaché case. Errol is rather attached to his dogs, he has three at the moment, and there was no way he was gonna let that pillar of society get away with it, no way, especially when he had a Heinekin bottle in his hand.

I used to have an Afghan, he told me later, who loved liquor. Really, darling, I used to take him to cocktail parties and he would absolutely wolf down my drinks. I wish I still had him, I'd probably be feeling a lot better tonight.

What happened to him? I asked.

Oh please, he said, with a characteristic sweep of his hair and roll of his eyes. That animal started pissing on my pillow every night. It really did get out of control, so I had to give him away. But listen darling, he is with a very wealthy family—winter in Beverly Hills, summer in Montauk, and I'm still doing the St. Mark's Place hustle.

—

*A*t first he seemed the keeper of dreams, the tender of fantasies. He would watch over the flames, stirring, kindling, making sure they never died out. With him, you could leave your illusions to be kept bright, burning, but under someone else's control.

It seemed so easy, so right, so seductive.

*W*hen I lived in Texas, Hal says, I was married. She was rich and pretty and we drove around in a little red MG. We had a kid and then we grew up. She still lives in Texas.

I moved to San Francisco, Hal says. I didn't have any money but it was warm and I took acid and learned how to steal food. I wasn't real happy then, but it was a hell of a lot better than going into my father-in-law's construction business in El Paso. I didn't write my wife or kid.

When I got tired of being broke I went to work driving a gypsy cab. That's when I started doing performance art. In my first piece, I drove a motorcycle with antlers on it into an auditorium. I had racing stripes painted down my back.

I met Lisa in art school there, he says, only she wasn't calling herself Lisa, she was going by the name of Cleo then. She was living with some Indian cat and wearing her hair in braids. He left her and moved back to the reservation and she cut off her braids and came to live with me.

We had a roommate who went crazy one night and threw forks out the window. Just forks. Somehow he managed to hit a cop and we all spent the night in jail.

I started doing canvases about that time and Lisa was singing in a band. I had a few things in some group shows. She had a few gigs. Things were alright.

I can't remember deciding to move to New York, Hal says. I guess we both just realized we had to. Everyone was doing it that year. It was like this. You could either get a job, get married, become a junkie, or move to New York. We moved.

*P*hil says this. Phil is Brett's friend. His partner, Brett calls him, his sidekick. Anyway, Phil says, there is one thing, one absolute, irrefutable truth. He says, You are either born cool, or you are not.

He says it is not something that you can learn to be. Oh, you may pick up a few pointers along the way, he says. You may study the walk, you may subscribe to all the right magazines, you may buy all the right records and go to all the right shows, but you cannot, you cannot change your birthright. You are cool, or you are not. And it is not contagious. You can hang out with cool people, but that will not make you cool, you will simply be someone who hangs out with cool people. You may go to all the right places, be invited to all the right parties, you may even have fucked all the right people. It doesn't matter, Phil says. The truth remains—you are cool, or you are not. And there's not a goddam thing that you can do about it. Right? Phil says.

*J*ohn's driving a limo now. John used to be married to a top fashion model and John used to grill burgers for a living and John has a father who is a well-known newscaster and who has offered to get him a job at the network and who picks up the tab for John's occasional dry-out spells in the hospital. But John is not interested.

He's driving a limo now and he says the work suits him just fine. He's good at talking to people and he's charming and so of course it makes sense that he would like it.

The other night, I heard a loud screech out the window and there was John making a U-turn in a silver limo. Mind if I use your bathroom, he said, coming in.

*S*ometimes, I bolt out of bed in the middle of the night and go into the studio, turn the lights up and stare at my paintings, like looking up your own name in the phone book for reassurance. And sometimes, it helps. Sometimes, I like what I see. Then I think, I am good, I am fucking good, and I go back to bed and fall asleep easily.

Other nights, I see only the flaws, the imbalances, the wrong colors. I find myself surrounded by taunting, medi-ocre images. Average, I conclude, nothing more than av-erage. And then I return to bed and think of getting a job or having another drink or of how long I can go on fooling myself and others before I am found out.

*M*y mother comes to visit me. I spend my whole life getting out of the slums, she says, and what do you do, you move right back down there. Would you mind explaining that to me, she says. Just what are you trying to prove? she asks.

It was gonna be like Paris / **9**

*H*is hand fit perfectly in the curve between my waist and hips, not merely resting there, but a hot and personable presence. My thumb was looped in the back of his jeans, my fingers spread across the taut swell of his ass. He leaned over and kissed me behind the ear. You ready for another drink? he asked. I looked at my glass sitting on the round stand-up table in front of us. Sure. Okay, I'll be right back. He ran his hand across my back and headed for the bar.

I watched the band setting up onstage, plugging in, testing drums, whispering to each other. He came up from behind, turning my head with a touch of cold glass, and kissed me on the lips. I opened my mouth, touching his tongue with mine, vaguely aware of the icy liquid that was dribbling over my shoulder and down into the V of my shirt, headed for the crevice between my breasts. We separated laughing. He put the drinks down after taking a sip from both, and traced the wet streak with his forefinger until it became lost in my bra. Then slowly he brought his finger to his mouth, wrapping his lips around it.

The band started to play. They're terrible, Brett said. Our thighs were touching, our arms were once again wrapped around each other. I kissed his cheek. Let's finish these drinks and get out of here, I said.

Forget the drinks, he said.

*T*his is Danny's story. I know it cause Danny had the bed next to Kim's in the hospital when Kim fractured his ankle. Danny had stringy brown hair and cracked white lips that he licked and licked. I figured him to be about thirty, worse off than Kim, all knotted up in wires and tubes, an arm here, a leg there. At first he would hardly say hello to me. Then one afternoon I sneaked in some scotch and the three of us got to drinking and talking and he told us his story.

He was, in fact, twenty-seven. He was going to be released in three days, though he would have to come every day for outpatient therapy. He would rather have stayed in the hospital, but they would not keep him. He had no place to go. He was scared. And he also hurt. But the doctors didn't want to give him too many painkillers. Him being a junkie for such a long time and all.

Anyway, this is his story. His father left him when he was four. Never heard from him again. He was raised haphazardly by his mother when she was home and sober, by his older sister, by the boys on the block. When he was nine, his uncle raped him. He shot up for the first time in tenth grade and got hooked real fast and stayed that way through four years of City College. Somehow, somehow, he managed to graduate with reasonably good grades, get himself to a rehabilitation center, kick heroin, after how many years, five, six, and go back to school on a scholarship to get a Master's in political science. He spent two years in the Southeast. His best friend there died of food poisoning. He returned to New York. His sister was knifed. His apartment burned down. He was mugged and beaten up while walking through one of the tunnels in Central Park. He was beginning to think of smack again. I mean really, man, wouldn't you? Oh god, he thought, just once, that's all, how good that would feel, sure would feel fucking good, but no, he thought, no, I won't, and just to make sure, he went back to the rehab center where he had originally kicked and started going to weekly therapy sessions. He was having a rough time getting a job too.

Then a couple of weeks ago, he ran into an old friend from his block in the Bronx, from his junkie days. He had some cocaine. Here, man, he said, take some, for old times' sake.

I kicked.

Aw, c'mon, a little coke won't hurt.

It wouldn't really hurt, he thought, it couldn't really hurt to do some coke, I mean it's not like it's smack or anything, he thought, so he took the foil and went back to his room.

Two days later, the landlady found him and called an ambulance. He had been lying in the same position, on top of his left leg and right arm all that time. They were permanently paralyzed. It had not been coke after all, but white Turkish heroin, a high percentage treat. His friend thought he was doing him a favor.

I gave Danny my phone number. Call me when you get out, I said, maybe I can help you find a place to stay. But he never did.

You believe all that? Kim asks me later.

Well, yeah, I think I do.

I don't think it's all possible, he says, not all of it. Never believe a junkie, he says.

*W*omen's art. Woman's art. That's what it is. Let's just say that's what it is. It is after all, isn't it? A woman making art is woman's art. And so it was and so it is and so it shall be.

So what's the problem honey? Look, you draw pictures of people. No macho-slapping-on-of-paint-abstract-expressionism here. Yes, this here is a fine example of woman's art.

Admit it. Now don't be difficult. Admit it, admit it. Why not?

*H*ow quickly it became a habit. One day there was no him and the next day there was only him. Only him. Obliterating all else, winding around anything that was not him until it either was him or was nothing.

How quickly everything became defined by him. By whether I was with him or was expecting to be with him or was not with him.

How quickly and easily and completely I gave myself up to it, how ready I was to be taken over by it, by him, him, him. Brett, Brett.

*S*he looks me up and down. I want to be friends with her. We have been friends for years, but not real friends. I like her. I want to be friends with her. She likes me. But still she looks me up and down. Her sister used to steal all of her boyfriends. She doesn't trust me. She thinks I'm out to steal her boyfriend. But I'm not. I want to be friends with her. She says, Yes, okay. But I can feel her looking me up and down when I turn around.

—

*F*orm. This is what was important to him. Substance was hardly a consideration. It was as if, in his wealth of finesse, he was somehow exempt from the necessity of giving proof of his creativity. No one questioned it. No one said, And what are you doing, Brett? And what are you working on, Brett?

And he in turn did not hold me accountable. With him there were no boundaries, no details. There were only eddies of color wrapping in and around us, vibrant, shimmering, shot through with gold.

He did not laugh at my fantasies, to dance nude with Matisse's ghost, to pour honey into a crystal goblet and set it by candlelight, he added to them, and together we created an environment of perfect beauty, of purple satin, of aesthetic anarchy.

Brett refused to see my doubts and my betrayals, and so they ceased to exist, at least for a little while. All was, Yes, of course. He did not sit me down when I spoke of painting and speak of dealers and critics and galleries. He did not ask for proof. He simply took it for granted that I created marvels. His was an effortless, unfettered belief.

*H*al reaches for another beer. My son is eight now, he says. He talks to me about his son. Hardly anyone else even knows he has one. I've only seen him twice since I split, he says. Sometimes my wife sends pictures. He's fat. I'm not much of a letter writer, he says, but I send him presents at Christmas and his birthday. Sometimes I think about bringing him east on one of his school vacations, but the loft doesn't even have full plumbing yet, and I wouldn't know what to do with him.

The last time I wrote my wife, Hal says, I couldn't find any paper, so I wrote on the backs of cancelled checks. She wrote back and asked if it was supposed to be art. What are you doing in New York anyway? she asked.

*O*ne says they are not emotional enough and one says that the emotion is so strong it is distressing and one says that they are too murky and that I should clean out my palette and one says she is struck by the vibrancy and one says the colors lack intensity and one says it is time that I took some slides around and one says that I should wait until I have a more cohesive body of work and one says this and one says that and I believe it all, for at least five minutes.

*H*e was always the loved one, the pet. He accepted this as one accepts socks for Christmas—he smiled, he said thank you, he stored it away. It was useful, it was sometimes lovely, it was to be expected. He barely took notice.

There were times, when, in a more pensive mood, he would wonder at others' desperation in love. Their motivations, though, remained beyond his comprehension. It was just another of life's little annoyances, to be avoided.

If he saw it in someone's eyes, that certain hunger that cannot be hidden, he was overcome by that mixture of pity and revulsion that others save for the sight of disease. And if he felt it in a lover's kisses, it was a signal for him to begin his graceful evasions, for he could slip away from love with the same enigmatic charm with which he courted it.

*L*ike a bird, she must have hollow bones, dry, brittle, fragile bones that would crack and splinter with a flick of the finger. Pale, pale skin and thin, yellow hair that wisps and frizzes as it wishes, electrified corn silk. There are often blisters around her mouth, large white bulbs of skin. Some say she has herpes. She does not mention them.

Her body, like her eyes, moves in rapid charged darts, now here, now there, nervous, incomplete. She eats with her face close to the plate, thrusting the fork back and forth between her open mouth and the food, ravenous, ravenous. She stops only to slip the ever-present bottle of vodka out of her purse and pour herself a healthy shot into a water glass, down it, and wipe her mouth with the back of her arm. It's just because I don't have any drugs right now, she says. Her nails are bitten to expose raw skin at the tips of her fingers, what's left she covers with iridescent gold polish.

Amy's boyfriend fractured his ankle a couple of weeks ago. She takes care of him. Together they design silk ties, hand-painting each one with a different pattern. They sell them to stores, they sell them to friends. Sometimes, they sell drugs. They pay the rent.

As soon as we get up the airfare, she says, we're moving to Amsterdam. This town is used up.

She pours herself another vodka.

ast month, Carrie got us both jobs as cocktail wait-
resses in a bar with a transvestite floor show. The place
seemed normal enough, in the business district downtown.
They had a pretty good lunch crowd, but the management
decided that what they needed to do was build up the evening trade and they figured the way to do this was put in
live entertainment and they decided on this transvestite act.
They figured it would be something of a novelty but nothing
hardcore like the forty-second street stuff. This would have
a little class. The act had played elsewhere and done okay.
They figured it was worth a try anyway.

The show consisted of six people and a phonograph. Five
white drag queens and a black man. Lip-syncing, or trying
to, depending on how many drinks they had had, to Judy
Garland, to songs from *A Chorus Line,* they churned and
slinked and sulked in varying amounts of sequins and eye-
liner and wigs. Except for the black man who did an in-
terpretive dance to a rhythmic drum track in only a G-string,
exhibiting the male body in its most polished perfection.

After the show, we would all hang out and have a couple
of drinks. The performers would change back into their
street clothes, usually skin-tight jeans and frilly shirts, unless
there was a party someplace that required a dressier look,
while Carrie and I finished cleaning up, collecting glasses,
and counting the money. Then we would all gather round
a big table and put our feet up and complain about how
tired we were and pretty soon, it would start, the stories
and the taunts and the teases, the gossip and the boasting.

The prettiest of them, Marlene, had thin chiseled legs and

narrow hips and long strawberry hair, though a man's back, always the man's back. She told this story.

I was wearing this new pair of heels, god were they beautiful—gold stilettos. It was last winter, remember that horrible snowstorm we had in February? Anyway, I was stepping out and I slipped on some ice. Honey, you should have seen me fly. I landed flat out. Well, I could no more get up, darling, what in my tight dress and those sky-high heels . . . well, it was something out of the movies, believe you me. Then I spot this guy walking towards me, a real macho piece of delight, and he comes up to me and offers me his hand, real gentleman-like. Honey, she said, I have never felt like so much of a lady as I did at that moment.

During our second week, Carrie and I went out on a break and didn't go back. Aside from tips being none too good, we both figured enough was enough.

*A*t twenty-one, he had inherited thirty thousand dollars. At twenty-two, he was broke. All that remained was a cracked-up Porsche and a taste for expensive wines and expensive drugs. And somehow, he remained able to satisfy those tastes despite his ever fluctuating funds. He was not above stealing if the opportunity presented itself. He always talked of scams. He was constantly in debt. But it never occurred to him to worry. There would always be someone there, after all, to lend him a few bucks, or to pay for his drinks, or to take him in for a few nights, right?

And he would do the same, for when he did have money, Brett was exceedingly generous. It was as easy for him to spend his own as to spend someone else's. He took real pleasure in treating whoever happened to be around to a lobster dinner. He insisted on bringing the most expensive wine to a party. He left joints in friends' mail boxes, cocaine in their noses. He threw loose change in the gutter when he didn't feel like carrying it. The next day, he would borrow money for cigarettes. It's only money after all, he would say, something will turn up, right?

At first, I begged him to worry. The landlord, Brett, I would say. Food, Brett, I would remind him, while he spoke of blowing one of his rare paychecks on a night at the Plaza. But he would only laugh. Don't be silly, why should I bother worrying? Look, if it makes you feel any better, you can do the worrying for me. I'll find something tomorrow.

And he always did find something, there always was money, not just money to eat, but money to go to cafés and to dealers, and I don't know how, I still don't know how.

That's not the point, I would say, his carefree smirk annoying me, the complete illogic of it frustrating me. What if there was no money? What if there was no one there to lend it to you?

But there always is, he would say, frustrated too.

*H*e needs space. Space. That's what he told me, that he needs space. Doreen twisted a shiny black corkscrew curl around and around her forefinger. We been together two fucking years and he wakes up one day and needs space. Okay, I say to him, I know we're on top of each other here and maybe we should try and find a bigger place. That's not it, he says. So I say, Look, you wanna go out every now and then without me, it's okay. But he says, No, you don't understand, I need space.

She twisted and twisted that curl. Another thing, he said he's never been sexually satisfied with me. I said, So why didn't you open your trap and tell me? He knew he was only my second man. So he didn't say much. That's what I'm doing with this here book, figured maybe I could learn something.

*M*mmmmm, he said, watching me get out of bed, my favorite Renoir. I frowned. What's the matter? he asked. All my life, I said, I've wanted to be a Picasso. Angular. I do not want to be a Renoir. But you're lovely, he said.

*D*o you ever wonder when it happens? Carrie asks. We are sitting on a couch at a party. She is wearing a white linen camisole. She is carefully made-up and her carefully streaked hair is carefully disheveled and she looks awfully pretty. I mean, when is the exact moment that it happens, when you start looking like that? We are talking about looking in a mirror when you get home, when your make-up is off or on in all the wrong places, when you are puffy and circled and not at all like how you thought you were. When do you think it happens? she asks. Is it the minute you leave your house? Halfway through the evening? Just as you walk in the door? When do you think it happens?

I had started working on self-portraits in the spring. Charcoals first, mostly bare outlines of what I might look like. I moved on to canvases after a couple of weeks, layered and thick. But I just couldn't get it right.

I got in the habit then of going to a nearby Woolworth's that had one of those photo booths, four for a dollar, waiting in line with the high-school kids and the lovers and the passport applicants and the people too stoned to do anything else. I did not, like them, giggle or groan or tear them up. I took them home and studied them, studied the serious expression on the grainy paper until I no longer knew who it was.

They didn't help.

I could sense it about to ring in my spine, feel it about to ring in my gnarled stomach, so tight, on the verge, waiting for the shock of that first ring, ring, goddam it, ring.

I'll give you a ring on Friday.

Ring, goddam it, ring, and don't be anyone else, don't you dare be anyone else asking if he's rung, cause I won't answer.

Maybe he lost my number, maybe he had to go away for the weekend, maybe . . . what's that . . . just the church bells.

Fuck the phone. Fuck its arrogant silence. Why won't you ring? I'll give it another hour, maybe two, and then . . .

Ring, goddam it, ring, surprise me, shock me, elate me, call me.

I washed my sheets for you, you asshole, and my hair. I shaved my underarms and my legs, even though I had just done it yesterday. I made myself pretty. You wouldn't believe how many outfits I tried on. I planned just what I'd say when you called, when you walked in, real casual, I almost forgot you were supposed to call, you know? And I emptied all the ashtrays and scrubbed the bathroom tub and removed the trashy novel from my bedside and you didn't even call, you asshole, why didn't you call?

*I*nsomnia. Fucking adrenalin at three in the morning. Not fed on simple fears, but apprehensions that enter the veins with the arrogance of cancer, leaving me too weak, too weary to get out of bed, or to read, or to watch television, or to paint, or to talk, to do anything but give in.

It's useless to try to outdistance it. As silly a notion as immortality. Oh, there are times when I almost outsmart it, falling asleep with relative ease. But no. At four or five, it shakes me awake, gripping me from the inside out, tickling my brain until I can't think straight, scratching the insides of my eyelids so they can't stay comfortably shut.

Like a two year old being denied what she most wants, I bang my fists and cry with frustration. Frustration that serves only to strengthen its enemy. Insomnia, of course, thrives on such futile emotions.

*T*ough little kid with the too big too dark eyes. It's her eyes, one man said, they're evil. Little girl grown up with too white skin and too much sex. Everyone wants her, her ten year old body and her full, full lips and her swaying black hair as she cocks her head.

I had anorexia once, Wendy says. I didn't get my period

for four years. After I got over that, I became a stripper. I used to have to take a lot before I got up there, but then I really got off on it. The lights and the rhythms and even all those disgusting men, I really got off on it. And it was at least a hundred bucks a night. Then I'd go back and make it with the owner's wife.

My husband's leaving me, Wendy says. She's crying. She's been crying for days. He's having an affair. I was having an affair too, but I didn't want that to end the marriage. I like being married.

And the man I'm having the affair with, he wants out too. I thought it was gonna be different with him. I'll tell you something. He's the first man I ever came with. Really. But he says it's gotten out of hand and he wants out. They always say that. It's gotten out of hand. They always want me at first, they want me real bad, and then they have me and then they say it's too much and they want out. I still don't understand it, Wendy says.

*B*rett was living in a rooming house on one of the seedier streets of the East Village. He had the basement room, thirty dollars a week, no windows. A double bed, a chipped yellow dresser, two paintings of roosters, and a stained olive carpet were part of the deal.

He had covered the naked light bulb in the center of the ceiling with multi-colored silk scarves, so that the room was washed over with diffused tints. His clothes spilled out of wicker baskets, arrogantly dripping onto the threadbare carpet. Scattered about were remnants of past lives, candles from Paris, photographs of himself on sunny beaches, drawings by friends taped neatly to the walls.

There were enamel pillboxes, an engraved cigarette case, numerous intriguing little containers. There were also empty bottles of wine, overflowing ashtrays, crumpled sheets, half-eaten croissants. It seemed like he could scoop it all up, throw it in the colorful baskets, and be gone in minutes, leaving behind no more or less of a mark than the previous tenants had. He never paid more than a week's rent at a time.

He never made excuses for the way he lived. He was not reticent about inviting someone to spend the night. He would buy a good vintage wine, drink straight from the bottle while sitting cross-legged on the bed that he had turned diagonally out into the room. He would show the way to the communal bathroom down the poorly lit hall, joke about the prostitute who lived next door, and then regale his guest with descriptions of his apartment in St. Germain, or the hut he had had in Negril. Not to impress, mind you, that was not Brett's intention. But simply to say, That's the way things used to be, this is the way it is now, so what. Things change, they'll change again. Maybe next week. That's the way it works, right?

*H*e wanted to hold my arms back and make me laugh at my feet running in place. He wanted to teach me to stop, to stop always pushing, pushing, for definitions, for reasons, for maps.

Sometimes, lying in bed, he would stroke my back and whisper, Relax, it really doesn't matter. And he would fall asleep while I kept running, running, tapping my fingers unconsciously in rhythm with the should I's? what if's? and he would close his hand around mine and try to make me still.

Most nights, he would just ignore me and go to sleep. But there were those when he couldn't, when he would wake and find me sitting up, biting my lip, when he would feel my restlessness seeping in, and he rebelled against the infiltration. Goddam it, he would growl, why can't you fucking sleep? Go into another room, go out, take a tuinal, do anything, but I'm tired. Can't you ever stop?

And more often than not, his brief tirade would wear him out, and he would be asleep again within minutes, leaving me to join him or not, whichever. It was my problem, after all.

*T*he hallway smells like piss. Cat piss, dog piss, human piss. Piss settled into the caulking between the stained gray and white tile floor, piss rotting the splintered handrail on the staircase, piss uncovered beneath the peeling paint.

But inside, it's okay, fine really. There's a small bedroom, a small kitchen, a small studio. A studio. A room for painting, a room no one has any business in, any business at all, but me.

Of course, there are paintings elsewhere, in the living room, in the bedroom. Others can look at those, they are finished, accepted. Let them look at those. But not the prenatal canvases. Not the room that holds the tools and the sketches, the plans and the half-creatures. There is not an open invitation to that room. That is mine. It's mine.

*T*erry is a family man. Not yet thirty, but a family man, a definite family man. Two young babies and a Nordic wife, a sculptor, and him a writer, short stories mostly, and they are a family, a definite family. Sometimes he brings the babies round, separately or together, well-behaved babies, too, which you tell him, of course, and he throws his head back and says, You should see them at home, and he rolls up his eyes and is pleased. Sometimes his wife sells some of her work, she has a gallery uptown, and then they are all right and sometimes she doesn't and he works delivering papers. Sometimes he seems sad and worried and talks of having to sell his car next week cause there's just no money, but then in a week, everything will be okay, or almost okay, and he will keep his car. And he keeps working on his stories. When I have enough for a collection, he says, then I'll get a publisher and everything will be okay.

In a couple of years, his children will be school age. His wife's parents have said, We will give you the money to send them to private schools. Terry says, We have never taken any money from them, but for that, we would. My wife's father is a survivalist, he says. He's building a house in the Ozarks. Of course, he would prefer that we decide to move there. He says it's the only safe place. But I don't think we will.

A snapshot of Brett. The fingers of his right hand stuck inside of his front jeans pocket, the inside of his arm arched out. His weight balanced on his left foot. The sleeves of his tan jacket pushed up above his elbows. The collar up. His hair, defying the laws of gravity, standing up on top. One eyebrow slightly raised.

I show it to my mother.

What is he rebelling against? she asks.

*S*weltering hot, hot, talking to Phil, distraught with sweat and hot, hot, summer, city, sickly hot.

Do you have anything? he asks out of habit, knowing the answer.

Nope. Not a thing.

I need some pills, he says. Three days, no booze, no pills, not even weed. Can you believe it? Look at me, I'm a joke, a flat joke. And this is supposed to be healthy. Oh, puhleese, he says. I swear, even the dealer went to the beach. I think I'm gonna be permanently damaged from this heat wave. Oh, my nerves.

Actually, I say, I've been trying to trim the drugs lately anyway. I've sort've been having trouble remembering stuff. It's got me a little worried.

What the hell do you want to remember days like this for?

I don't know, but . . .

But what? You're not doing anything anyway. You can't in this weather. And you call this living. I'm walking around half dead. I need some pills.

I know.

Who can we call?

I don't know.

*S*ometimes, Brett stays in and reads French novels. In French. He particularly likes the late nineteenth century.

*Y*ou know that guy I told you about? Carrie says, the one I slept with last week? Well, he called me last night at four in the morning. He said he needed to talk. He said he was going back to France. He was saying something about having two lives, one there, and one here, with me. He kept on asking if I understood what he was talking about. Of course I didn't understand. I mean, I understood, his English is pretty good, but I didn't understand. I mean, we've only seen each other twice for Christ's sake, and he's talking about a life together. Really. All I really cared about was whether he had found the earring I left behind. It's not just for fun, he says, like the things you read about in magazines. It is special with you. Carrie affects a French accent à la Maurice Chevalier. So then he tells me he did a little cocaine. Now, I know for a fact that he has never done any cocaine before, and I could have told him that it was just the coke that was making him need to talk, but he never would have believed me, not the way he was going on. I'm not high, he says, I hope you don't think that's why I called. Then he started in apologizing for waking me up.

So then he says, How was it for you? Shit, I didn't know what to say, I mean, what kind of question is that? Nice, I say. Nice, he says, and starts laughing. Christ, I would've been willing to forget the damn earring if I could just have pretended the whole thing never happened.

But he wouldn't give it up. It's like this jazz, he says, and he puts the receiver to the speaker. I waited. Do you know what I mean? he asks. All I could think of was how much I hate abstract jazz. So I say, No, I don't know what you mean, which was a mistake, cause then he starts to explain, and the more he explains, the less I understand, until I just stopped listening completely. I kept thinking, He means well, he means well, but I was pretty pissed off, especially when he started saying something like how being with me had something to do with enjoying the total New York Experience. Can you dig that? Carrie says, the New York Experience. I told him to stick to postcards.

*W*orking in a void. Painting without feedback. It is difficult to maintain a belief in potential when there is seemingly no progress, no good news.

*M*y first impulse was to worry, to worry frantically. It didn't matter that his friends had warned me about it, about his penchant for disappearing for days at a time only to resurface without the barest sketch of an explanation. People didn't do things like that, I thought, and even if they did, he certainly wouldn't do that to me.

But of course, he did. He was supposed to meet me at three and he wasn't there and he wasn't anywhere, then, later, the next day. I thought of his ability to fall into trouble. I thought of his ability to fall into someone else's arms. And I panicked.

I called Phil. He wasn't worried. He's taking drugs, he said, he's laying low. And then the panic subsided and I only despised him. And I never wanted to see him again. And I wanted desperately to see him so that I could tell him that.

He shrugged his shoulders. I had things to take care of, he says. You could have called, I say. No, no I couldn't have. He didn't understand what all the fuss was about. I'm here, aren't I? he asks. You could at least tell me where you were. I told you, he says, I was out.

I learned two very important things from him. Nothing is irrevocable. Know when you are finished.

When I was paralyzed by the fear of marring the superlative perfection of a blindingly white virgin canvas, he would make me scrawl all over it in a pastel wash. Humanize it, he would say, you can deal with flaws.

And when I ruined emotion by fussing over detail, when I insisted on overstatement, when I could not let go, he would say, Have faith, it is done.

He was a good teacher, a damn good teacher.

And I was in love with him.

Every now and then, he used to invite the class to his loft in Soho for coffee. We would sit on the floor amid the cans, tubes and brushes, so different from the well-guarded neutrality of home, and listen to his anecdotes of painters he had known, his talk of galleries and parties.

I longed to pose nude for him, to have him put down his brush and make wild love to me, to have him gather me up into his enchanted world. In my flushed adolescent manner, I kidded him about it. First of all, he said, you are underage.

And second of all, he said, you know I only do abstracts. And he chuckled and squeezed my shoulder.

*B*rett collected people. Even he wasn't always sure how it happened. It just did. Often he would start out for some-place alone and arrive with a burgeoning eclectic entourage. It just happened.

If he didn't remember each one's name, he was sure to remember their story. If it amused him. And if not, he made one up. Casually, almost imperceptibly, he would choose the most minute detail of one's life and embellish it until it glowed with intrigue and romance. Even the subject did not question it. Brett could not stand to be surrounded by boring people.

*S*he had been living with him for two years. No, I'm not going to marry him, she says, he doesn't like going out to dinner. How could I marry someone who doesn't like going out to dinner? I'm just living with him, she says, in much the same way that an actress or a painter will say, I'm waitressing, instead of I am a waitress. It's only tem-porary, after all. Nothing to get used to, god knows.

*H*al is looking at the girls going up and down the stair-case. He likes girls, he likes girls more than anyone I have ever met. Girls in short skirts and girls in pants, girls with long frizzy hair and skinny girls and beautiful fashion girls and girls with thick ankles. He just likes girls.

This wouldn't be a good time to have an affair, he says. I'd get too excited. I can only have an affair when things are going well between Lisa and me. Then it doesn't affect us.

Lisa says I'm an overgrown adolescent, he says. She keeps asking when I'm going to grow up. I'm just having fun, he says. You know?

*W*ith each act of evasion, of thoughtlessness and irresponsibility, with each new proof of his seeming insensitivity, my determination grew. I would reach him. I would be the one. I would make him see. That other women had thought exactly this and failed was irrelevant. I would succeed. I would be the one.

With a lover's blind optimism, with that peculiarly feminine commitment to the omnipotence of love, I saw only what waited for me one step, just one step beyond his façade of carelessness. More than anything else, I believed in my ability to change him, and I clung to this with single-minded stubbornness even when he did not call or show up or when he was too inebriated for it to matter, when he was Brett. It was only a matter of time, I thought, time and patience. He will wake up one day, and I will be the one. I will be the one.

*H*e was older than me, and in some circles, considered an Important Artist, or at least someone who would in the long run be considered an Important Artist. He had a gallery, he had had reviews in the major art magazines, the expensive glossy ones. He had a good deal.

So when it came time to move some of the larger canvases from his loft to the storage space he had rented around the corner, he didn't think that he should be seen doing the carrying. He had an image to keep up, after all. He offered Brett and me a hundred bucks to do it for him.

You're being ridiculous, I said.

Shut up, Brett muttered. It's easy money.

I shut up. It only took us one day. Easy money.

I saw him from a block away. I considered crossing to the other side of the street so I wouldn't have to see him, but I didn't. He was sitting cross-legged on the pavement leaning up against the red wall of the shop. He was wearing new blue jeans and a leather jacket. His eyes, squinting in the sharp morning sun, were focused on his feet. Sweat dripped from his wavy blond hair down his sallow face.

Aren't you hot, John? I asked. Well, yes, I guess I am, he said, carefully taking off his jacket so as not to disturb the whiskey bottle that was sticking out of one of the pockets. I'm waiting for them to open, he said. I'm dying for a coffee milkshake. Been thinking about it for hours. Care to join me? he asked. No, thanks, I said, I have to go pick up my laundry. Well, have a nice day, he said, maybe I'll bring the limo round later.

I'm going to check out this new location, Brett said. Locations. Like tumors, no sooner did the cops get rid of one than another would spring up. Of course. And no matter how fast they opened, closed, shifted, someone always knew where one was, some junkie always knew, word always got out. Of course. There's a new location, good stuff. So of course, Brett went.

I heard the gunshots, three, dull unmistakable thuds, on the sidestreet, but I couldn't see anything out the window. Anonymous shots, no screams, no questions.

Shit, Brett said, panting, sweating. This city's getting crazier all the time.

*N*one of us went to Woodstock. Though every now and then we watch the movie on television. All that long hair and mud and LSD. Pathetic, Brett says, and changes the channel.

*F*etal position, with the covers pulled tightly over my head, that's how I sleep best. It gives me freedom, freedom to dream without inundation, the freedom of safety.

His weight tripled in sleep. Sprawled on his stomach, the bed became his domain. Often, he would fall across me, a dead man. Then I would lie still, though strangling, unwilling to disturb him.

Once, he says, I had a girlfriend who slept hunched up on her hands and knees, a nervous dog. She had hair like yours. She smoked Marlboros and chewed Juicy Fruit and ate speed. She was older than you. She always thought there were bugs. You'll be just like her, he says, in a few years, you'll be just like her.

No, I say, I could never sleep hunched up on my hands and knees, a nervous dog.

A Millet exhibit at the Metropolitan. It was raining and I could almost smell the dank earth and the sweat of the peasants settle on the marble floors. I was sad. Melancholy, that's the word, I was melancholy. I guess maybe it was because I was in love, or jealous, or lonely, something like that. But those stooped bodies, those lined faces, too much musk.

*H*e ordered my first martini for me, frowning with disappointment when I shivered at the first sip, smiling like a proud father when I ordered my third.

You must always buy two bottles of champagne at once, Brett said. If you drink champagne at night, then you simply must have it in the morning. Yes. Of course.

*D*iane tells stories. She is a story-teller, an oral traditionalist. I have a telling on Wednesday, she will say. And I always want to go, of course, but I never seem to get there. Getting there seems to be a problem. So I listen instead to the stories she tells about everyday things, the things we all talk about.

It's such an old story, she says, I'm embarrassed to tell it. I want to hear, I say. She tells her story. She was the oldest of nine children. Nine. Can you imagine. For as long as she can remember, her mother was either pregnant or sick or both. Diane had the responsibility of taking care of each new addition, as well as the previous ones, while her mother was busy working on the next and her father was busy doing double shifts at the factory trying to support them all. Nine children. So by the age of eighteen, she had had quite enough of listening to her brothers' and sisters' problems and dispensing bandaids and hating her parents and so she got married. He was my first boyfriend, she says, my first friend, really. I never had much time for friends. Anyway, I thought it would be much better to live with him than to live at home and so I married him.

He was going to college, which was something to be proud of, a college man, so I said, I'll support you while you go to college. We had a one room apartment and he was gone during the day and being as how I worked nights, I had the apartment to myself all day and I was happier than I had ever been. Then he finished college and I was glad because by that time I was tired of night shifts screwing the tops on bottles and I thought now he would be making some money and it would be my turn to go to college. But he came home after graduation and he had gotten a good job and he said, I think we should start a family now. He thought I would be thrilled, he really thought that would make me happy. I told him I thought I might like going to college myself, and he said there was no need for that. I had never told him that I didn't ever want children, he would never have married me if I told him that, so I didn't. But now I did. At first he thought I couldn't possibly be serious and then he said,

But you don't have to have nine, and he tried everything he could, he said, That's impossible, every woman wants children, and I said, But I don't. When he finally realized I was serious, he asked me for a divorce. I already had my bags packed. I was ready to move to New York.

Now I have my story-telling, she says, and I'm taking a few classes at night. I'm even dating. I never went out on a date in my life before. And you know, she says, I'm happy. It never occurred to me that I might be, but I am. By the way, she says, I have a telling on Tuesday. You should come.

*F*ingerpainting. God how I used to love fingerpainting. The plastic smell of the little jars of paint, the tops always caked with flaking color, and the paint itself, the gloppy shiny plastic thickness, the cool cool slime between your fingers, how I loved that, feeling the paint between my fingers, whirling it round and round on wet paper with my fingertips, making scratch marks through the puddles of paint. I really did love it. You always have the messiest painting, a teacher said to me. And you always end up with more in your hair than anyone else in the class. It was just that I loved the feel of that paint so much.

*T*here is a march and then a rally midtown in support of nuclear disarmament. Few of us go.

—

It is impossible to even imagine such a catastrophe, they tell us.

In fact, we cannot imagine stopping it.

Oh my nerves, Phil says.

A heavy hazy morning. The kind that promises a day of thick unbearable heat, or at best, rain, but discomfort either way. We were lying under a tree in Washington Square Park—it seemed as good a place as any. I was lying on my stomach, aimlessly pulling at blades of grass, wanting to taste one or two, but fearful of what might have been there before me. He was lying still, watching the slow drunken movement of the bloated clouds. We hadn't spoken since we had decided on a place to rest.

Then quietly, as if I wasn't supposed to overhear him, he said, I need a métier. I turned to him, but his eyes remained fixed on the sky. It was another voice that had spoken, one that Brett did not often let me hear, and I feared that if I questioned it, if I tried to push it into conversation, it would return to silence. So I said nothing, waiting for him to continue.

The next time he spoke, it was the other, the casual voice, saying, I think we should get going.

*C*arrie has a younger brother, David. He reads Schopenhauer for kicks, she says. We're not a whole lot alike. He has a habit of calling me up for my opinion on his latest detached analysis of his latest nervous breakdown and then ending up telling me I'm frittering my life away. Frittering? I ask. Frittering, she says.

Carrie also has an older brother, Kenny. He used to be beautiful, Carrie says. Now he doesn't look as good as he used to, only no one's told him. He still thinks he can get away with the same things he did when he was a little younger. He calls me up every now and then for money.

We don't see each other all that often, she says. David thinks Kenny and I are superficial and boring and Kenny thinks David is pretentious and boring and he just thinks I'm kind of useless and then there's my mother running around, saying, I do wish you children were closer, and my father who won't forgive any of us for not wanting to take over his business. I hate holidays, Carrie says.

*T*hey had it all mapped out. They had carefully planned for my successes, my victories. I would have every advantage, every benefit they had never had. They had the best of intentions.

They spent two thousand a year for me to fingerpaint in the most desirable of playschools, and taped my masterpieces to the refrigerator door. They gave me private music lessons, dance classes, European tours.

And when they were angry with me, for whatever the reason of the moment might be, they would yell, We never asked you to feel guilty because of what we have given you, because of the sacrifices we have made. You're so goddamned unappreciative. And I didn't feel guilty, it never occurred to me that I should, except perhaps for my lack of guilt. None of it had been my choice, after all.

And in more affectionate moments, on special occasions, graduations, birthdays, New Years, they would say, You are a special child, a blessed child. You will take what we have given you and succeed. We have faith in you.

But a painter, dear? With your background? It must be just a stage.

*S*he sat like a child, with her thick legs straight out in front of her, her toes pointed up and out. She wore many layers, despite the fact that the day was no cooler than any other in July in New York. She had spread before her her Sunday brunch—a fresh jar of stuffed olives, a can of sardines, a pack of Players cigarettes. As I walked by her, she put her hand over the jar of olives, either to show that she was not sharing or to protect them from my high-heeled feet.

I am at a point where I must dive in and come out with some sort of structure, and I can't. I just don't seem able to do it. Maybe I'm not serious enough, maybe I'm not talented enough, maybe I'm not a painter after all.

But what then? What then?

It's my only chance.

*W*e stayed until closing time, when the lights are switched up white and harsh and brutal, and then we walked a few blocks west to a late night restaurant. He had had too much, way too much, of whatever. Even he knew that. More than once I had to stop him from wandering into moving traffic. He promised me that he would have coffee when we got there. I know, he said, I know, I know.

We found a table and sat across from each other. A glass of white wine, I said to the waitress. Scotch, he said. Brett, I said, you were gonna have coffee, remember? Oh yeah, I forgot. He shifted his eyes slightly toward the waitress. I'll have coffee and a grilled cheese sandwich, he said.

His head was resting on his hand, close to the table. He was talking about horseback riding, about how much he used to love to ride on the wooded paths in Pennsylvania, about how that was exactly what we should do tomorrow, that's exactly what we should do. The waitress put our drinks in front of us. He reached over and took three sugar packets out of the holder. He always took three sugars. He opened the first and slowly poured it out, watching, entranced. It missed the cup. He opened the second and poured that too right next to the cup. And then the third. There was a pyramid now of white granules an inch from the mug. Brett, I said, can't you see what you're doing? He blinked and looked at the table. Oh yeah, he said, and reached for another three packets.

The waitress came with his sandwich. He opened it, poured ketchup on the cheese, closed it and picked it up with both hands, bringing it gradually toward his face. He was unable to stop the motion, though, and it fell over his shoulder and onto the floor. He turned to look at it, shook his head, and smiled.

Maybe we should get a check, he said.

*E*conomic collapse. Phil is in a frenzy. Total and complete economic collapse, he is saying. That's what this guy on television was predicting last night. He said there was gonna be rioting in the streets for food. No more social security, no more welfare, no jobs, no nothing. Can you believe it? And I don't even have a hit single yet. What am I gonna do? Eat guitar strings? Oh, my nerves.

*H*is mother lived in New Mexico, his father in Pennsylvania. They had been divorced for twelve, maybe thirteen years. They had never gotten along. He was an executive in some large company and he took his job very seriously, very seriously. It had something to do with computers. He was analytical by nature, not an emotional man, tightly wound. He expected nothing short of perfection from himself and his family, always. There were a couple of times, though, when things seemed to get beyond him, when he could not control the course of everything about him as he thought he should. Then he would start to make lists. Lists of goals, lists of groceries, lists of his wife's faults, lists for his children's lives, lists for anything within reach, and especially lists for anything that wasn't. After the lists came the numbers. Sentences of numbers, digits, and nothing else. Then he would go away for a few weeks. A rest, they said, a rest. It happened like that three times before Brett was eighteen.

His mother was silent through most of his childhood. She

spoke to her husband as little as possible. She did not work, she raised a family, rarely talking to any of her children either. Then she left. She had had enough. Now she was living with a thirty year old man in a trailer in New Mexico. She would not take alimony. They lived on welfare. She had bad arthritis that often kept her in bed for days at a time. When she was up to it, she would type long letters to her children. She would expound the virtues of Marxism. She would rail against marriage in general, hers specifically, as a particularly evil capitalistic institution. She would send her love. Sometimes she would include diffident pleas for money.

It was around eleven and we were sitting in a brightly lit coffee shop having breakfast. It was the first time Brett had spoken of his family in anything more than vague allusions or flippant references. He had in his hand the latest of his mother's letters. It had been in his pocket, unopened, for days. He hadn't been in the mood. Now he opened it and unfolded what turned out to be a xeroxed copy of an article on how to raise children with a properly Marxist value structure. At the end, she had scrawled, I wish I had done a better job. I love you anyway, Dora. There was a phone number. Brett scanned the piece of paper and handed it over to me for perusal.

When was the last time you talked to her? I asked.

I don't know, he said, a year or so, I guess. Last time I called, all she did was cry, for fifteen fucking minutes. Then she asked for money, like I really have any extra cash to send her.

Didn't you ever tell her you went through the money?

Why bother? I started to once, but she only hears what she wants to hear and that isn't it, so I gave it up. Look, she's okay. I mean, she's a little crazy, but she's a lot hipper than my father, anyway.

Don't you ever miss her?

Yeah, but . . .

Why don't you call her?

He finished his toast without saying anything. He went to the cashier, got a couple of bucks' worth of change and went to the phone booth to call New Mexico. I ordered some more coffee and played with the pack of cigarettes he had left behind, trying to imagine Brett, the son, talking to his mother.

Well? I asked as he sat down.

She's alright. I woke her up. She said her legs have been hurting, but having sex seems to help. Listen, he said, I don't feel like doing much today. Let's get some wine and go back to your place.

Je t'aime, he says. He is saying I love you, I think, he is saying he loves me. *Je t'aime,* he says it again. He has said it before—*Je t'aime.* But never in English. Never I love you.

*H*is dreadlocks were piled high under a yellow, red, and black crocheted hat. He was wearing short, short white track shorts and a white T-shirt. He had long muscular legs. You couldn't help but notice them. They were magnificent. We had seen each other around. We had smiled at each other. Now we were talking.

I am a recording artist, mon, he says, his voice lilting and flowing with his Jamaican accent. I do construction work, too, studio time takes bread, you know, mon. I like you very much, he says, talking faster than his rasta lingo permitted but in time with his new york rap.

I've seen your girlfriend, I say, she's beautiful.

She is that, he says, but a man can have more than one woman. Would you enjoy going and smoking some herb?

I did not look at his magnificent legs. I don't think so, I said. Not tonight, anyway.

He laughed and started to walk away. Goodnight, darlin, he said, this dread is going to bed.

I wasn't exactly sure why I was angry with him. Perhaps it was simply because of how quickly he had fallen asleep, how easily and irrevocably he had deserted me in favor of his tuinal-induced slumber. And how there wasn't a goddam thing I could do about it.

I cried. Propped up in the corner of the bed, I sobbed as loud as I could without sounding completely ridiculous, stopping now and then between sobs to stare in growing frustration at his motionless body. Seeing that my tears would have no effect, I got out of bed and got the bottle of Smirnoff's from the freezer, and returned to my corner, drinking with a vengeance straight from the bottle. I lit a cigarette and put the ashtray on his stomach, but even when I ground out the butt, he didn't budge. He must have taken more than his usual dosage.

I drank until the rise and fall of his stomach, as imperceptible as it had been a few minutes ago, began to make me dizzy. Then I went to the bathroom to splash cold water on my face and ended up lying down and falling asleep on the cool tile floor.

Waking up a few hours later, I was thankful that he had not wandered in and found me there, sprawled out on the floor like a common drunk. And I was furious that he hadn't. I returned to bed, finding him in exactly the same position he was in when I had left. He didn't feel me climb in beside him.

The alarm went off about an hour later, and as he reached over to shut it off, he gave me a peck on the forehead and asked if I'd had pleasant dreams. Sure baby, I answered. He began to fondle my breasts. I had a headache. You better get up or you'll be late for work, I said, turning my back to him. He tried to insinuate his leg between mine, but I remained still. I heard him mumble something along the lines of cold bitch as he got out of bed.

*P*hil was forming a band. Another one. The last one broke up when the bass player made it with the drummer's girlfriend and the drummer stole the bass player's amp and sold it to a friend visiting from Boston. Women, Phil says, you can always trace it to a goddam woman.

Phil asked Brett to join. Brett had wandered in and out of bands for the last year or so, but nothing much had come of it. C'mon, Phil said, isn't that why you came to New York to begin with? It'll be perfect, Phil said, we like the same kind of music and we'll do it right this time, we'll get real tight, and I've got some connections now. We'll hit it, Phil said, I know we will.

Brett didn't need too much convincing. It sounded good. And after all, Phil was right, that is why he had come to New York. Wasn't it? Of course. Sure, he said, why not?

*J*ohn stepped out of the limo, a long black sleek number this time, with a white cardboard silver-handled take-out container of Chinese food. Mind if I have dinner here? he asked. You had to like him, you just had to, there was no way around it. Have a beer, John. Don't mind if I do, he said.

*W*hen she was about twelve, Patty discovered things hidden under her parents' mattress. Dirty books and crotchless panties and bras with holes for nipples. Things like that. I used to sleep over at her house, and when her parents went out, we would read aloud from the books and laugh and wonder why on earth anyone would want the other kind of stuff.

Her father used to go away on business trips. Who did you see? Patty would ask. Hanky Panky, he would say. For years, Patty thought Hanky Panky was a client her father had lunch with in San Francisco. Then she got older.

I've never heard them like this, she whispered into the phone late one night. She keeps yelling, I'm not going to have it in me if it was in someone else. Do you think they'll get a divorce? Patty asked. It seemed like a lot of parents were getting divorced that year.

There were other covert phone calls. I did it, she whispered one night. I did it, I whispered another night, a couple of years later. She had already done it with the boy I did it with. Don't worry, she said, there's better.

*Y*ou don't mind if I clean up a little, do you? Carrie asks. Of course not. She was putting away a mass of records that lay strewn about the floor. They have to be in alphabetical order, she says. While putting something away in the M's, she pulls one out. Remember me telling you about Greg? she asks. Of course. Greg was, according to Carrie, the great love of her life, there would never be another like Greg.

When we were separating our things, she says, I went upstairs to take the sheets off the bed, and he said, I'll stay downstairs and do the records, and I said okay. When I got to my new apartment that night, I went to play this album, it had been a favorite of his, and do you know what that fucker had done? He had given me the cover but taken the album out. She bent it this way and that for emphasis. I've always kept it though, she says, and puts it back in order.

*T*his is what Phil says about the great love of his past. I went away for a while and she wrote me a letter saying we should be together again and she loved me and blah blah blah and I went home. And when I got there, I could tell by her eyes that she did not want me there, even though she did make love to me that first night, I could tell that she really did not want me. So the next morning, I said to her, What's wrong? and she said, It's not you, it's just that

I'm not into the idea of a relationship anymore. I need to be alone, she said. Can you believe it? But you said you loved me, I said to her. But that was weeks ago, she said. Can you believe it? Women.

I woke in the middle of the night. I looked at him sleeping. His face resting, peaceful, lovely. I wanted to reach over and trace his eyes, his nose, his lips with my fingers, but I didn't want to wake him. I wanted only to watch and to treasure him and to marvel at having him beside me, to want him to sleep forever so that I could sit and watch and protect him.

*L*ocal luminary, semi-legendary junkie rocker stumbles out of the dressing room at the top of the stairs. Hey man, he yells, or rather mumbles as loud as he can through his junk haze, to the employee at the bottom of the stairs, there's a girl up here who needs help getting down the stairs.

Employee, friend, colleague, babysitter, answers in an exasperated but still amused voice, You got her that way, you get her down.

No one emerges.

I feared that he would grow bored with me, that I would become one more in his repertoire of adequate lovers and he would begin to grow restless for novel erotic experiences.

I would buy crimson satin sheets and down pillows for my bed. I would put a mauve bulb in the light overhead and spray perfume on the mattress. I would put a bottle of deep rich burgundy and two crystal goblets on the nightstand.

I would seduce him as Eve would seduce a jaded Adam, beckoning him to enter a new Paradise, a tropic ripe with experience, a bordello filled with a gilded past. I would offer to fulfill his every fantasy, I would second-guess his libido. I would please him in ways no one ever had, I would tempt and addict him to me, I would equal the hold he had on me.

I just want to please you, I said as I slowly unbuttoned his shirt and unzipped his jeans. He never wore underwear. His penis, lying against his stomach, reached to my tongue as I gave it teasing flicks and long strokes. I just want to please you. Tell me, anything you want, tell me.

And you? he asked. What about your fantasies and desires? What do you want?

I could feel my muscles tighten. It wasn't just that I was seeking to mold myself to his imagination, or that I would lose the edge I was seeking to gain by making myself vulnerable as he asked. I had never been able to comfortably express my needs or wishes in sex. I had always had to struggle painfully for the words *slower* or *here* to get out of my throat, and more often than not, they remained unspoken while I lay silently hoping for the best.

I was so much more comfortable in the world of his desire, where I had only to respond to his lead and the risk and the responsibility for the rules were his. I was more abandoned under Brett's caresses than I had ever been, but the times when he asked How or Where still left me stuttering, embarrassed. For all the times I had lain in muted anger at men who hadn't asked or cared, I felt more pain the times he did.

Another night, I said.

Now, he said.

Yes, now.

*G*od is he dashing. I could easily be in love with him. Easily. With his dark Mexican skin and his dark Mexican hair and his broad shoulders and his tall dashing figure, dashing, dashing, lunch here, weekends there, at only the best houses, of course, and he is poor, mind you, always poor, but dashing and kind. He is that too. He is too old not to be kind, to be just dashing.

He too is an artist. He paints planes, in the air, taking off, landing. Sometimes he builds them, sewing them out of sturdy cloth with big clumsy stitches and then he hangs them with thick string from the ceiling.

He has worked for a long time, for too long, as a busboy in a restaurant. Too long. He is getting too old for that, don't you think? So he is studying the antiques business privately with a man he met last summer on Fire Island. Eighteenth century antiques. He goes to auctions with this man and he goes to his home with his notebook and he tries to learn, and in return, he sometimes types. In return, he says, what I really do is go out to dinner with him. He likes being seen with me. And I listen to him, he likes talking, and I try to get him to talk about antiques, but that seems to bore him. It's beginning to take up too much time, he says, since I don't really think he's serious about teaching me the business after all. I don't know, he says, it seemed like such a good bet.

*J*eez, Hal says, arching his back away from the metal chair, that's cold. You sure you can do it? he asks.

Sure. Relax.

Careful, he cautions as the tips of the scissors accidentally nip his ear.

Sorry, I say, go on with what you were saying. His skin is icy smooth, so soft. The deepening violet circles under his eyes, the creases that linger after a smile, these remind me that he is thirty-three after all. It would be easy to forget.

What was I talking about? Hal asks. Oh yeah, Lisa. I think the answer is for us to keep separate schedules since we can't afford to live separately. His gold tooth catches the light. I comb and cut. Did I ever tell you I tried being gay? he asks. About five years ago, he says. I thought maybe that would be the answer. But it didn't work. I like women.

I've noticed, I say.

Finished. I start brushing off his back with a towel, then take a blow dryer to the more persistent hairs.

He stands up and looks in the mirror. He runs his hand through the right side of his hair, blunt and even just below chin length, and then the left side, a quarter of an inch long. He uses the mirror to view the back, where the short and long peak in the center.

You sure that's what you wanted? I ask.

Sure, he says. It's perfect.

━━━

*P*hil says they're gonna be playing Madison Square Garden within two years. Phil says there's no question about it, they're gonna be better than the Rolling Stones ever were. Aren't you being just a little conceited, I say. Not conceited, he says, just convinced.

*W*e were all high. I don't remember what we took. But whatever it was, we must have taken quite a bit, cause we were all real high. Somewhere along the line, it must have been in the last bar we were in, we had picked up Reggie. Or Reggie had picked us up. Anyway, he had now become part of our group, like it or not. Reggie. He? Did I say he? He was a she. Or vice versa. Or something. I didn't know. I don't know now and I most certainly didn't know then.

Where are you from? I asked Reggie. I was curious. He had such a strange accent. I am from Paradise, he said. Oh, I said. And then, a few minutes later, I had forgotten where he had said he was from and I wanted to know. Where are you from? I asked again. And once again, he said, Paradise. I am from Paradise. And later, as if I had still not heard, I said, Reggie, where are you from? He told you, they yelled at me, laughing. He is from Paradise.

After walking around with Reggie for a while, we decided that we didn't much like him. Reggie, isn't it time you went home now? But he just laughed at us and kept right on. And we couldn't very well go home, cause none of us wanted Reggie in our homes, so we kept on walking along with Reggie until we were all very tired. Brett nodded to a cab that was coming and whispered, Run, and we all ran, and poor Reggie didn't run fast enough. Hurry, Brett said to the driver, and as the cab took off, I lurched forward and chipped my front tooth on the divider.

Kim called the next day. We shouldn't have run like that, he said, it was mean. Besides, he said, I thought she was pretty. Oh, Kim, I said, she was a man. No! Yes. Well, he said, I did think there was something a little strange when he kept saying he was from Paradise.

*W*hy did you first want me? I asked.

Because you looked caught up and separate, he said. I wondered if you were talented.

In painting or in bed?

Both.

*O*ne says, All you ever talk about is death. And the other says, What would you like me to talk about? And the one thinks about it for a minute and says, Actually, I had a dream about it. Last night, I had this dream where I died. I was at my own burial. Well, how were the arrangements? the other asks. Oh, really nice, the one says, fabulous flowers. That's good, anyway, the other says, what say we get a check?

I leaned over gingerly to see if he was awake yet. He was lying on his back perfectly still. A few renegade tears were slowly making their way down his cheeks. I pushed a strand of hair off his forehead. What's the matter? I asked.

He turned to me and started to wipe the tears away. Nothing, he said, smiling a little, just one of those mornings.

I kissed his brow. What is it?

Nothing. He shuddered with annoyance.

Nothing, he said emphatically.

*D*o you remember the bicentennial?

Of course, she laughed, I was bi that year too.

I tried not to look too shocked. But Marcia? Marcia? You're kidding.

No, really, she said, I was having an affair with a woman that year. Oh, you are shocked.

No, just a little surprised.

Copywriter Marcia who calls her mother twice a week and observes Yom Kippur and took a share in a house in Westhampton because she thought the chances were good there of meeting the right man. Of course I was surprised.

What happened? I asked.

This woman and I were working together, she said, and we started going out together after work. I didn't give it any thought, but then one night, she reached over and kissed me and it was the most wonderful kiss I ever felt. So we had an affair.

It was very nice, but I'm not the type that could last like that. There was no future. We couldn't even sit in a movie theater with our arms around each other. At least I couldn't. I never regret it though, it was lovely. Oh, you are shocked.

No I'm not.

*A*s close as we came, as hard as we tried, he still wasn't mine. That's what kept me so hungry for him. I'd never be satisfied until I was sure that his love wasn't just a whim that he offered at will or convenience, until I could close my hand around something more substantial than a promise.

We had banged against each other, rocked with each other. And still we separated. Now I would have him wrap around me like a cobra, tighter, harder, I would have him enter and lick my guts with his wicked tongue until I dissolved in flames. Like a cat greedily slurping up every last drop of milk, I would gulp him down and then lick the bowl searching for more.

*C*arrie was jangled, all exposed nerves and dangling energy. Mark went to Nashville for the week. Mark was her new boyfriend. Mark went to Nashville for the week to take some of his tapes around down there. To see if he could be a country-western singer. Or to see if he could be a country-western songwriter. He went to Nashville for the week with another woman.

Just friends, Carrie keeps saying, I know they're just friends. She wrote some of the songs with him. She had to go. But shit, she says, they're gonna be down there in Nashville for a week with adjoining rooms. You wanna know what his horoscope for today says? I'll tell you what it says. It says, Contact with someone of the opposite sex will light sparks. He's got three more days to be just friends with her, Carrie says. He damn well better not come back with sparks for anyone but me.

*W*e were sitting on the floor in my living room. Brett and Phil and me. The fans were whirring, an occasional firecracker—left over from the Fourth of July—exploded outside, reggae played softly on the stereo. We were drinking ice tea. Phil and I were talking.

Brett made no sign of hearing any of our stilted conversation. His lower lip was tucked beneath his front teeth, his eyebrows were raised high into his forehead. I've got to go out for a few minutes, he said. C'mon Phil, we'll be back in fifteen minutes.

They were at the door before I could say anything. Bring me back a pack of cigarettes, I yelled after them, as if that would guarantee their return.

I put on a new album and washed out a few cups and other dishes that had piled up in the sink. I fiddled with a stray paint brush. I wondered if he would come back in fifteen minutes, in a few days.

When they did return, they did not stop to chat or offer any explanations, but went straight to the bathroom and locked the door. I stared out the window.

Phil came out first, pulling the door shut behind him. I stayed by the window and waited, counting cars, counting minutes. Finally I went and knocked on the bathroom door. Brett?

Just a minute, Sugar.

I went back to the window. I had lost count.

When he came out, his previous look of distracted impatience was replaced by a syrupy benevolent smile. Gone was the tense biting of his lips. What's the matter, Sugar? he asked.

What's going on?

He laughed indulgently. Don't worry, it's clean in there.

I don't care about the goddam bathroom, I yelled as I saw him push the syringe deeper into his pocket.

Look, he said calmly, if you want us to leave, we will.

It's a little late for that, I said.

*T*he thing I like about your work, she is telling me, is that it's obvious you don't think much.

Huh?

I mean, she says, you can tell that you just paint, you don't sit around and intellectualize about it. You just paint. Right? You're not a thinker.

Right, I say, of course.

*H*e seems so much older than the rest of us. But he isn't. Maybe it's because he owns the club. Or because he is married. And he lives in the suburbs. And his wife is pregnant with their second child. Maybe it's because of all that and the way he looks, older, loose and soft, with his nylon shirts and his stomach bulging out and sideways over the pants that are belted too low. He must be older than the rest of us, he seems so, so certain, so, so ... as if there could be nothing that he hasn't already decided. And we are his wayward children. We who are in fact his contemporaries, are his wayward children. And he will gossip with us and laugh at our antics and sometimes, he comes too close and says slyly, Married men make better lovers, you know, and you laugh and he laughs cause he's just joking after all, and you ask about his son, the football player, he calls him, so you call him that too. How is the football player doing? you ask, because you know he likes being asked, and you like asking cause you are curious, you are curious about this man who is like you and yet so unlike you, could you really have grown up at the same time?

And sometimes he takes you up to his office and says, That guy is no good for you, he's no good, I didn't want to tell you this, but I saw him in the bathroom before and he was sweating bullets, green as they come, sick from something, he's into something hard. Get rid of him, he says, find yourself a nice doctor or something and settle down. And you say, Yeah, and he looks concerned, honestly concerned, which makes you a little sad, except that he is also looking down your shirt.

And sometimes, he takes you up to the office and gives you cocaine, and he likes taking it out and putting it on the mirror and making neat even little lines with the razorblade he keeps in the top left hand drawer of his desk, and he likes giving it to you and you like doing it and then when you go downstairs, he will give you delighted knowing looks for the rest of the evening. There are nights, of course, when you would like for him to give it to you and after hinting around for a while, you say, Hey, Jeff, you have any coke tonight? and he will shake his head, no, his wayward child.

And sometimes you even feel like going up to his office to talk, just to talk, but he's too busy, having to run a club and all, so you just say, So how is the football player doing? and he smiles and says, Fine, fine.

I'm sorry, Sugar, he said. He had forgotten to call when he said he would. Again. He had forgotten for twenty-four hours. I really am sorry. You know I meant to. Don't be angry, Sugar, I'm trying to change, really. You're the first woman I've ever wanted to change for, really. Come give me a kiss. That's better. Just be a little patient with me, okay? Okay, Sugar?

*O*nce, in college, I took LSD and I didn't talk for ten hours. I wrote my name. I thought I was strangling and every time I thought I was strangling, I wrote my name. I saw Julie turn into a witch. And into an old old woman with a decrepit face. I saw her very ugly, hideous, and I could never see her the same again. A witch. I looked out the window and I saw men dancing in leering circles with knives but they did not scare me. They were not there for me.

At first, I was going down steps and I couldn't tell if I was going fast or slow. Am I going fast or slow? I asked Bob. Bob had given me the LSD. That was the last thing I said. Then the walls started swaying in rhythm with the music. And the fire said Fire. The others were chopping wood for the fire and I thought they were going to chop me. Take that axe and chop me. I was terrified then. A boy who was studying math stood up and said something in trigonometry. They were all speaking foreign languages that I couldn't understand. Someone would come over and say something to me and I could either not hear or not understand. A sound barrier. But what could I say. See, only Bob knew about the LSD. Only he knew. The others didn't. And it was important, it was crucial that they didn't find out. They must not know. They must not know. They must not know. I don't remember why anymore.

I took LSD again but only with other people who also took it and then we all knew, we all knew absolutely everything then, of course.

*I*t will be better there, she says. See that's what I always think, that it will be better there. So I always go. Only this time, Carrie says, I can't. I just can't run this time, she says. I mean, first of all, I don't have any money. No tickets in my back pocket. Nothing.

You know, Carrie says, I've left most of my lovers when they were asleep. It's easier that way. I can't stand hopeless situations. There's always the next corner, the next man. Only this time I can't. And I don't have any valiums either, she says.

*I*t was a respite. We were comfortable. Nothing important to be said. I will change. And I will change. You did this. Only because you did that. Let's do this. None of that. No recriminations. No promises. We watched re-runs of the "Mary Tyler Moore" show. We laughed at the jokes. We had a perfectly fine evening.

*H*e had money and he was going to take me out to dinner. Someplace special. We were going to get dressed and make an evening of it. It was even his idea. I'll pick you up at eight, he said.

I stretched out the ritual of getting dressed as much as possible. A long bath, a new way of pinning up my hair, make-up, perfume, an old, black, strapless dress. And it was still only seven-thirty. A glass of wine.

He was late, but that was to be expected, he was never on time, never anyone else's, anyway.

Nine o'clock.

More wine, more cigarettes.

He called at eleven. He was in a bar, a noisy one. He had run into some old friends. Why don't you come meet us, Sugar, he says, you'd like them.

*P*hil's father is an alcoholic. Not a patrician alcoholic who cares just a little too much for his highballs. And not a Bowery drunk who has that and only that. Somewhere in between. That's where his father is. He's given up trying to have a job, gave that up years ago. Why bother, he says. He was once a high school principal. Don't miss those damn kids, he says, not at all. It's been a while. He's living in a housing project now. He collects welfare. Why not, he says, I sure as hell paid my dues.

I should never have gone to see him, Phil says, it's too hard on my nerves.

*L*arry says artists should not have to work. Artists should make art and people should pay them to do it and that should be that.

Larry is pretty. He has thin hips and thick auburn hair and eyelashes. He has managed to live, to live well, without working, for years. He has an understanding boyfriend who pays the rent. He has parents who buy a painting every now and then for a few thousand dollars. And when I have my first show, he says, then I'll have some real money.

He knows the right people, they'll pay the right price. He doesn't even understand why an artist would ever consider working. You have too much pride, he says.

I offered to let them use my apartment as a dressing room before the gig. I figured they would only be over for an hour or so. Brett came early. I made him a grilled cheese sandwich while he ironed the mauve shirt he planned on wearing. He took a couple of bites and asked for a glass of wine. He said he didn't feel like eating. Not that he was nervous or anything. He just wasn't hungry. Then Phil came. Then Pedro. And then Kim. The band. And then some. There was Tony and his brother Ken. Kids. They had volunteered to be roadies for the night. Setting up equipment and the like. And there was Kim's girlfriend, Amy. And some others whose names and functions I never quite grasped. There were the bottles. Jack Daniels. Wine. Tequila. There were the shifts in the bathroom.

We made it home by five. Just Brett and me. Tired and

drunk. We agreed that the evening had been a success and went to bed. In a few minutes there was a knock on the door. Tony and a girl. Is Brett here? he asks. He's sleeping. Tony took this as an invitation to go back to the bedroom and wake him up. Hey man, he said as he shook the foot of the bed, you mind if we crash here tonight? Sure, Brett mumbled.

Tony went out to tell the girl it was okay. You a painter? he asked as he noticed the canvases leaning against the wall.

Yeah.

That's nice. You want some J.D.?

No thanks. I'll get you some pillows.

While I went looking for extra pillows, they turned the stereo on. The windows shook with the beat of an early Who album. It was beginning to get light out. Brett came out of the bedroom. He lit a cigarette and took a long swallow from the bottle offered him.

Another knock on the door. You get it, I said, I'm sure it's not for me.

Phil entered, red-eyed, scowling. Let me see that bottle, he said and sat down.

Are you expecting anyone else? I asked Brett.

Who knows, he said. I'm exhausted, I'm going back to bed.

Do me a favor, I said to the group sitting on the floor, just keep the stereo down, okay?

We woke up around twelve the next day. Phil was sleeping in a chair. Tony and his girl were in the shower. There were two more people I had never seen before talking in the studio. Brett was hungry. I'm gonna run across the street for something to eat, he said.

I could tell by his eyes that he would be gone for days.

Let's get some beer, one of the guys suggested. Brett split, I told them. What's the matter, you two have a fight? Tony asked. I turned to Phil. I'd appreciate it if you'd all clear out of here, I said. Phil stood up obligingly. C'mon, he said to his acquaintances, let's get out of here. They grumbled as they gathered their things.

*M*aggie is three years old. She is Terry's oldest child. I don't spend too much time with children, but I do like spending time with Maggie.

Maggie and Terry and I were sitting in Terry's living room and Maggie climbed off her father's lap and pranced in her toe-first prance over to the piano and climbed up on the bench and put her hands, her little hands, on the keys and sat there and looked at them and looked at them. Finally, Terry said, What are you doing? I am looking for a song, Maggie said. Of course.

I'm only really jealous if they're younger than me. It's okay if they're more productive, if they have a gallery, even if they're rich and famous. It's okay if they have more lovers, or a husband, okay if they get invited to all the top openings and know what to say once they get there. It's okay, because in time, I'm going to have all that. So, it's all okay. As long as they're not younger than me.

—

*W*e woke up sticking to each other and cranky. The sheets, the backs of our necks, everything was damp with night sweat, stale and bothersome. You know what we need, he said, we need a cool bubble bath and bloody marys. That would do the trick. I didn't think anything would do the trick, but he was in a playful mood, and his childlike enthusiasm could still be charming.

I picked my kimono up off the floor and went into the kitchen to fix the drinks, using the two good wine glasses I had left from what was once a set of eight. He ran the bath, pouring at least half a box of citrus powder under the tepid water. How do you feel about the Supremes this morning? he yelled across the hall. I hadn't yet considered the Supremes. Whatever you want, I answered. Coming out of the kitchen, I saw him dismantling the stereo from the studio, unhooking speakers, unplugging the receiver, and carrying it piece by piece into the bathroom. Grab this, he said, nodding to the album that was sliding off the amplifier as he passed by.

We lay at opposite ends of the tub, resting our drinks on the rim, and sent little plastic boats that he had bought the week before back and forth. Stop! In the Name of Love bounced around the tile walls. The phone rang. Shit, he said, I knew I forgot something.

*T*im says he's getting married. He's not exactly sure when, but real soon. He said not to tell anyone, but he told everyone, so it's really not a secret. He's been with his girl for three years and they love each other and even though he flirts more than anyone I know, he really doesn't mean it. It just comes naturally.

They both want to have kids and they're both over thirty, so it's definitely a consideration, but they're not sure if they will. He's a performance artist and she's a dancer and he's a cook and she's a waitress and neither can foresee making any kind of money in the near future so they don't know how they could afford it. They could afford it, I mean I'm sure the kid would eat and all, but Tim says he doesn't want to be like those old hippy families that you see, with the father in baggy old pants and the mother in thrift-shop and the kid in clothes that are always either too big or too small. He says he never wants to be in a position where someone can pity him. So they're not sure about the kid.

Tim has an open face. Those spread apart kind of features and translucent skin that never seems to show any imprint of age or hurt or even fatigue. The kind of face you trust. Midwestern and sweet and sincerely friendly.

*T*hey played at some club in New Jersey. It was inconvenient, but they were guaranteed enough money to make it worth their while. I didn't go. Kim's account of the night went something like this.

When we finished playing, I walked back to stash my guitar and I nearly tripped on 'em. I look down and see Pedro's brown ass goin' up and down, so of course, I bend closer to see who's underneath. It was this chick who'd been hangin' out by the door all night, this blond thing with real tight pants. She was nothin' great, but she had real big tits, and she looked ready, you know? So anyway, by the time he's finished, we were all back there, not doin' much but hangin' out and watching. He climbs off her and she just lies there wiping herself and lookin' up at us. Look, you gotta remember, it was the end of the night and we were all fucked up and Christ, I don't know how the rest got started. Anyway, she wanted it, shit, she was laughing the whole time, you know there are girls like that. I guess we all fucked her at some point and then I think someone shook up a coke bottle and put it up her—made a mess, but she didn't complain, and then she gave, well, she gave someone a blow job, but he said it was only fair. So anyway, the club owner, this fat, bald jerk-off, came back to pay us. Man, you shoulda seen the look on his face. He just stood there staring at us for a few minutes and then he gave us the bread and told us to get the hell out. So we packed our shit and split. The girl? Oh, we gave her a lift home.

*S*he used to be taller than me and she's not anymore. She used to be wilder, more daring. She lied to her parents more, fucked more, she cut more classes. She was going to be a great writer and live in Paris. And I was going to go with her and paint. She's a traffic manager now in an advertising company. She doesn't care much about her career. It pays the rent. It passes the time. She is reasonably happy.

In the past few years, we've seen each other only for lunch. Once a month. We haven't seen each other's latest apartments or met each other's latest lovers. We don't go to the same parties or clubs. We wear different kinds of shoes. We keep different kinds of hours. We look forward to our lunches.

We talk of having children. We talk of moving to Vermont. We talk of new shampoos and sometimes of being thirteen again. We talk about our families. We talk about each other and we talk about sex and we talk about love. We don't talk much about politics or art or even movies. We talk about quitting smoking. We catch up. We forget the names that are important to our separate lives, but somehow we remember the importance. Once a month.

*I*n the middle of one of his disappearances, he left this note in my mailbox: sad songs okay, *je t'aime,* B.

There was no way to reach him.

*T*hey were married for seven years. It wasn't a particularly good marriage or a particularly bad marriage, it wasn't one that you tended to give much thought to.

But they had problems. Sexual problems. He didn't make love to her. Couldn't get it up. He blamed it on her. You're too aggressive, he told her, it turns me off. She stopped kissing him. He didn't like it when she made overtures. One night he said to her, I'm having an affair. She wondered what this other woman did that she could not. It's with a man, he said. It's not the first. I slept with men before I married you. I thought you would make it different, but you didn't.

They divorced.

*E*very time we said goodbye, if only for an hour, a day, a night, every time, I thought, I might not see him again.

Every time, I watched his back as he walked away, or turned around to see if he was still there. Any parting kiss could be the last kiss. He did disappear, after all. He could disappear permanently. Who knew. Who knew with Brett.

*W*ith the flash insight and the urgency to communicate it, with the immediate need to express and be understood, with the explosive clarity of cocaine, I knew that I understood him. Perfectly, shiningly, absolutely. And I had to let him know. That was all I wanted him to understand. That was everything.

And so I called him and he said hello and I said hello and I said, I just want you to know, I understand you. Oh, he said. If a voice could shrug, that's what his was doing. I really do, I said. Do you understand that? Do you understand? I understand you. Anything else? he asked. That's all, I said.

*M*y name was supposed to be on the guest list. Each member of the band was allowed two names and mine was supposed to be one of them. Brett would see to that.

The people who guard the doors, those omnipotent safe-keepers of style, have heard it all before. I know someone. I am someone. I work for something. They've heard it all before and all that matters is if your name is on the list in front of them or not. Cut and dried and please don't make a scene.

Mine wasn't, of course.

Look, I said to the zoot-suited man on the stool, my boy-friend is the guitar player in the band. He just forgot. Why don't you let me go in and get him. He'll come and straighten the whole thing out.

If he was your boyfriend, honey, he wouldn't have for-gotten to put your name on the list, now would he?

As I was about to begin trying to explain the quirks of Brett's personality to this disinterested man, Phil came out to check on something.

Ask him, I said.

She's alright, Phil said.

With a grudging nod, he let me pass. I headed straight for the dressing room. Brett was perched on a table, tuning his guitar. Why wasn't my name on the list, I demanded. Oh, I forgot, he said, without bothering to look up. Why don't you go get yourself a drink or something, he said, handing me some free drink tickets. I don't have time to talk right now. He went on twisting keys.

*O*n stage, he looked something like a punk Van Gogh, all cheekbones and live-wired hair. Wild and haunted and vulnerable. He took to it naturally.

*B*ig Vinnie died, and Hell's Angels came from all over the country for the funeral, and of course, the wake. About two hundred of them. Big Vinnie was one of the more no-torious brothers. I used to see him around now and then. He was the fattest motherfucker and covered with tattoos on every visible inch of his body, except his face. Even his hands had tattoos.

Lizabeth, my sister, was visiting. She didn't particularly like coming to my neighborhood, but she came anyway. I'll come see your work, she said. That morning, all two hundred Angels got on their bikes and, after interminable revving up, rode to the funeral home, which was around the corner. We had to stop talking and put our hands over our ears. The windows shook drastically and a plant fell off the table.

Does this happen often? Lizabeth asked, trying to sound calm and polite, thinking, after all, that it might. She took her pocketbook to the bathroom. A valium.

Lizabeth married an architect named Greg and they live in Westchester. She is trying to get pregnant. I'm sure Greg has some friends we could introduce you to, she says, coming out of the bathroom.

Big Vinnie died of diabetes. They buried him along with his motorcycle and then they painted the front of an abandoned building on the block. In Memoriam, it says. Big Vinnie. 1948–1981. The Beast from the East.

*E*veryone wants to know what my excuse is, Carrie says. She is not in a good mood. Since when did you need a goddam excuse to live here? she asks. I'm damned every way I turn. I'm not an artist, I don't have a career, and I'm not married. Three strikes. What really kills me, Carrie says, is if I tell people I don't really do much of anything, they don't believe me, they think I must be holding out on them or something. Sometimes I really hate New York, Carrie says. I don't know, Carrie says, maybe I did have an excuse. I mean, I must have. Everyone here does. Right?

*T*he perfect state of drunkenness—numbness. One drink away from sentimentality, one drink past caring—almost, almost past caring. I don't care, do you hear me? I don't fucking care. I don't. I think I will have another drink. What the hell should I stay sober for? Certainly not for you. So what. So fucking what. I used to think there were people shooting arrows into my brain, poisoned arrows. I would see them, those warriors with their taut bows, once I shrieked all night, in fear, in pain, because those arrows were so real. And I prayed. I don't know to who or what, but I fucking prayed for it to stop, and it did, eventually, and they never came back. So what the hell should I stay sober for? Another time, when I was much younger, I used to think there was a little man sitting on my brain like a workman on a roof, directing me, telling me what was right and wrong, scolding me when I tried to get away with anything. I was very moral then, very moral indeed, that little asshole wouldn't even let me litter. But he too went away eventually. So what the hell should I stay sober for? Out of fear? Christ, I ought to be past that by now, don't you think? Hope? Out of hope that there just might be some reason to stay somewhat ... I think I'll have another drink. What the hell should I stay sober for?

*H*e came over with a bag full of groceries and told me to go out for a few minutes and when I came back, there was a quiche in the oven and wine in the refrigerator and candles on the table. And he took pleasure in setting the table and serving the dinner and it felt like we were a couple. A couple who had dinner together and then made love and didn't have a single problem. It felt like that for a few hours.

*C*athy told me this story. Cathy is studying to be a midwife. It is about her adviser her freshman year. Cathy said she was a very nice woman, very friendly and cheerful, the type it is okay to have as an adviser. She wasn't that much older than the women she advised, maybe eight or ten years.

Once this woman had been a year away from being a certified midwife. Just one year away. She had taken her books with her one morning to the laundromat. It was midterms week. She looked up from the text and noticed that the water wasn't sudsing as much as it should. Perhaps she hadn't put enough detergent in. She opened the machine to add more. Suddenly, the cycle started up with violent rotations. She was too shocked to scream. By the time someone came to help her, it was too late. Her right arm was severed at the elbow.

So she advised people. And only to the advisees who asked did she tell this story.

Cathy asked.

*G*randma scrubbed other people's floors for a living. And she never complained. Not even in Russian. That's what my mother says. Then she went home at night and scoured her own floors.

I can't remember ever seeing my mother cleaning the floor. I can't even imagine it. Not on her hands and knees. She buys the Ajax and gives it to the maid and leaves the house. She has more important things to do, after all.

*B*rett was depressed. He had been working for the past two weeks driving a truck delivering flowers. It gets so frustrating, he says, having to work full time and go to rehearsals and still try to find time to do anything else. There are times when I get an idea for a song, a good idea, and I don't have time to write it down and then I forget it. It's ridiculous to have to work when you have better things to do. Do you know what I mean? he asks doubtfully.

What the hell do you think I've been doing for the past couple of years? I was incredulous.

I guess so, he says.

*H*e was a punk back when punks were punks. Safety pins and bondage gear and chains. Remember those? He still wears them. And he wears, too, a limp, the result of a fight one night in a Bowery bar back when punk was punk.

He wears the limp proudly, a war veteran, to be treated with respect, a leather green beret. And sometimes, like an old world war two vet, he sits and drinks beers and reminisces about the good old days, the brawls and the bars and the bands, the good old days, back when punk was punk.

A couple of years ago, I took a course in post-Impressionist art. It was quite informative. Among other things, the teacher said that even though Toulouse-Lautrec had stunted deformed legs, he was a favorite among the prostitutes in Montmartre. It seems he had a rather large penis. That's what the professor said, anyway.

C'mon, he says, you can tell me. Did you ever make it with the two of them?

The two of them he is referring to are Carrie and Mark. They are a couple. We are close, we really are. We have not made it together. All he knows is that we are close.

Oh, c'mon, he says, haven't they even asked you to make it with them? C'mon, you can tell me.

*W*ouldn't you like to put on just a bit of lipstick? my mother asks as I am getting ready to leave. It upsets her to think of me crossing the city without a bit of lipstick on. But then, she is upset in general today. You know I don't like to compare you and your sister, she says, but I would like to see you settled.

Are you sure you wouldn't like to meet Jim? she asks. Jim is the son of a friend of hers, a lawyer with a top corporate firm, and only twenty-eight. And a nice-looking young man too, she says. There's no harm in meeting him, now is there?

But mother, I have a boyfriend.

Low-life.

But you haven't even met him.

Listen darling, she says, don't you think it's time you started going out with a different breed of man? There is no future with struggling artists, especially if you insist on being one yourself. Hang out with low-life and all you will meet is low-life, she says. Now why don't I just have a little dinner and invite you and Jim.

No.

Well, will you at least do me one favor?

What is it?

Will you at least put on a bit of lipstick before you leave?

Sure.

There. Now don't you feel better?

*T*his was to be their big night. The guest list was filled with names—Atlantic, Polydor, Mercury, Warner Bros. The first three rows were reserved for the A & R men. They were all coming. This is it, Phil says, I can just feel it, we're gonna get signed tonight. This is the night. A three-record contract, European tours, limousines, I can just feel it. This is the night. Oh, my nerves.

Keep Brett straight, Phil says to me, no record company is gonna sign a junkie.

Except for a couple of beers, Brett stays voluntarily sober. Did you see the list, Sugar? he asks. We're going to kill them tonight, Sugar, he says, tomorrow we'll quit our jobs.

They went on forty-five minutes late. They were waiting for the first three rows to fill up. On his way back to the dressing room after his final look, Phil reported, Secretaries. All any of them did was send a couple of fucking secretaries. Gave the girls a free night out, that's what they did.

Ten minutes after the set, Brett was out on the street, looking to score.

*C*aught up in the self-perpetuating malaise of not getting any place but stoned. Even the rehearsals that he had been so enthusiastic about just a few weeks ago were now passed over, forgotten, ignored. He no longer deemed them important. He no longer needed them.

If he did manage to go, he was late, he was high, he was sardonic and petulant. Or he was too strung out to be anything. That's what they told me. Sometimes they, usually Phil, called to complain to me. As if I could influence his behavior. Sometimes they called looking for him. And if I said I had no idea where he was, they thought I was covering up for him. As if when he disappeared, it wasn't as much from me as from them.

Rehearsal time was expensive and they had a couple of important gigs coming up and Brett had trouble remembering the words to the songs as it was, they said. Brett said he had it all down pat. He said they were wasting time with adolescent power plays and trying to upstage each other and they weren't writing anything new and interesting and he liked playing with them, but rehearsals were in general a waste of time. Brett said Phil was becoming quite a pain in the ass, getting self-righteous and all, and losing his sense of humor. They're just not experimental enough, he said. He's just too undependable, they said.

—

I remember. It was spring. Just spring. We bought a new album, we turned the volume up loud. It was good. A bass beat deep pop jump-around good. He was wearing new sneakers and it was late afternoon and no one was home and I wanted to make love—jump around new sneakers new spring new love—that's what I wanted. Only we weren't making love then. It was morally wrong. And too dangerous. I don't think we should, he said, and I had to agree with him, or I would have been morally wrong. But that late afternoon, the music was louder than my conscience. Maybe we should go out for ice cream, he said, which was morally correct, but hardly satisfying.

*H*e came over late. I had put on a slinky nightgown. I had chilled champagne. He was bored. It was not new to him. We listened to music, drank, chatted. We didn't kiss, we barely even touched. By the end of the bottle, we were fucking on the floor.

When the record ended, he slid out of me, turned the album over, returned to my womb, and resumed humping. A, B, C.

You seem to have trouble coming, he said.

*T*hat moment when everything assumes the translucence and clarity of a perfect diamond, when exhilaration pours through the veins, flooding the spine and brain with imperatives, I can do it, I want to, do it all, when energy plays havoc with reason and all must be done at once, at once, for time is jolting with menacing speed, and there might not be enough time or speed to do it all. The flash of amphetamine when the encompassing thought is only this—more, more speed, now, and when more speed doesn't bring the bursts of potential that it did last night or the night before, but instead rushes one toward the crashing exhaustion that inevitably greets one after too much speed, when the body is past the satiation point of positivity, and energy itself turns rancid, when the running of feet and nerves is no longer toward action but a desperate attempt to outrun reaction, to fill the stillness that is the gateway of creeping depression and overwhelming fear, so that action becomes a goal in itself. That moment when body and perception rebel, when everything quivers with distortion and absurdity and there is no energy left to stave off the shaking and no courage to succumb to sleep. When eyes ache from sight, and hours, nights and days, have blurred to this moment, this terrible burnt-out moment, the culmination of too much speed, when all that remains of potential is the bitter taste of anxiety.

*J*ohn gives Hal part of his paycheck each Friday. That way he won't spend it on liquor or drugs or whatever it is that will make him broke by Sunday, and without rent money by the end of the month. Hal keeps a special account for him. Often, by Monday or Tuesday, John will go to Hal and say, Hey, man, can you lend me ten bucks?

The other night, Brett gave me ninety dollars. Do me a favor, Sugar, he said, and hide it. And don't give it to me til next week. I put it in a box of stale Rice Krispies.

He came back later that evening. I need the money, he said. But I thought I wasn't supposed to give it to you until next week, I said. Don't you need it for rent? Just give me the money, he said. And of course I did. It was his money after all.

The next day, he is angry. Why the hell did you give me the money, he says. I told you not to.

*A*n uptown cocktail party in honor of a downtown artist's first show. I'll go if you go, I say to Carrie. The downtown artist is a mutual friend. Her boyfriend is not. The ultimate sleaze monger, Carrie says. Please, I beg, you can't make me go by myself. Okay, okay, Carrie says. You think there'll be food?

We each kiss the boyfriend on the cheek. Just ask a Negro for a drink, he says, looking over our shoulders to see if perhaps there is someone more important behind us. Our friend is surrounded by an impenetrable circle of art world personalities. We head for the bar.

We sit on the ledge of a corner window. We are high up above the west side. Even the McDonald's below us seems somehow shinier. The room is filled with white rugs and magnolias and gossip about people we do not know. The servants have taken a liking to us. They keep our glasses full. Who says it doesn't pay to have influential friends, Carrie says. Our friend comes to visit us in our corner. I'm sorry I can't talk right now, she says, I'm busy selling.

You'd think they could have at least sprung for hors d'oeuvres, Carrie says as we take the subway downtown to get something to eat.

*Y*ou see, he says, I believed the lyrics. Brett in a reflective mood. Really, I did. I remember when I was a kid and I hated everything and I would go and lock myself in my room and listen to some songs and they said that I was right, that it was right to hate everything. I believed all that, he says. Believed in the outcast life, believed all that rock'n'roll romance. I really did believe there could be another way. Brett in a confessional mood. I believed the lyrics, and look. It's nothing like that at all. Brett laughing. There are no more gypsies. Brett being honest. Nothing thrills me anymore.

I love you, he whispered in my ear. I love you. Oh, god, I love you, I whispered back. We stayed up all night, whispering, I love you, I love you. We went to sleep in the sunlight. Damn birds, he said.

Sugar, he said the next morning, I can't find my wallet, have you seen it? I looked, but I couldn't find it either. Maybe you left it at Phil's, I said. We were at Phil's last night? he asked curiously. Don't you remember? No, he said, I don't remember much of anything that happened last night. Were we really there?

*S*o he calls me up one afternoon and says he's in New York for a few days to try to sell a script for a musical he's written and he's got Big Appointments and Big Plans and they're putting him up in a Big Hotel and would I like to meet him for a drink. And I say sure and give him my address. Being a native New Yorker, I'm sure he grimaces. And I clean up my apartment and put on high heels and look forward to seeing him—he used to have a talent for making me laugh.

He is deep brown and he has cut off his black curls and shaved his beard, only a well-trimmed mustache remains. He wears sunglasses, even though the bar I take him to, a chicer one than I usually habituate, is by no means bright. He speaks almost exclusively of his project. He is serious now. I no longer feel free to tease him the way I used to. He is bisexual now. He is diplomatic. He has grown up. I remember when we used to steal fruit together to eat in the park. It really wasn't all that long ago.

He wants to know if I have a tape deck—he has a cassette of the music. It's fantastic. I have to hear it. Much to his surprise, I don't. We move on to another bar down the street, one that plays cabaret music over a cassette system, a place with a beautifully hammered copper bar, and an out-of-work actor working behind it. Yes, he will put the tape on.

He drinks expensive scotch. I drink Remy. I figure he'll pick up the tab, after all. It's difficult to hear the lyrics over the chatter of the attractive clientele, but I compliment him on the melodic quality, which is in fact, quite good. We split the bill. I sneak back to add a few dollars on to the tip.

Afterwards, we go on to one last bar, where he explains deals, points, and percentages. We're both slightly, well, perhaps more than slightly drunk by now. Over our final drinks of the evening, he tells me confidentially that I really should move out to L.A. I have connections, he says, I could help you get a job in the art department of one of the studios. Haven't I had enough, after all? He seems to feel a bit sorry for me. I promise him I will think it over. We kiss goodbye. On both cheeks, of course.

A confusion and dissatisfaction deeper than who I am or am not sleeping with. An unhappiness caused by more than loneliness.

My time and energy swallowed up by day to day, night to night living—I have not touched a canvas in weeks.

*I*t is the end of the day. Across the street, Sereena is sweeping the floor of Sereena's Candy Store. Carrie comes in with a blossoming geranium. Here, she says, stick it in your window or something. I could use some coffee, she says.

Listen, Carrie says, I'm going to tell you what I think and then I promise I won't mention it again. Your boyfriend is a turd. I can't stand to see what's happening to you. Sara, I know his type. He'll run you down.

But Carrie, I say, he's not like that. We're beginning to work things out. Really we are.

He's an addict, she says, you can't work things out with an addict. You should know that.

He's different. And anyway, he's not an addict.

Who are you kidding.

Drop it, Carrie.

Promise me you'll think about it.

Okay, I say, but you're wrong.

One more thing, she says. Your hands haven't been exactly covered with paint lately. Now how about that coffee.

*J*ust think what a gas it will be, Brett says, the ultimate drug. We have been talking about senility. Imagine, he says, being able to fade in and out like that, a permanent nod, without any of the hassles. No connections, no excuses. That's what I call freedom, he says. It might even be worth getting old for.

*H*ow can you do it? I ask.
Do what? he asks.
Make yourself so numb.
I may become numb, he says, but never immune.

*W*hy can't I be busy just once? Just once when he calls, why can't I say that I'm busy. I've made other plans for the evening. I want to work on this painting. I feel like being alone tonight. Why can't I say no. Just once.

*O*ne thing he never did—he never offered me junk. Never even asked if I was curious. Not like an alcoholic who needs a buddy knocking 'em back one for one. And it wasn't because of greed, not the drug greed that inevitably turns trust inside out. It was because he needed me to stay clean, a foil to his waywardness.

Junkies, at least in the seminal stages, are prone to saviors and missionaries, prey to women in love who believe in miracle cures. It's an occupational hazard.

And it's easy to play. As easy as answering the phone in the middle of the night, and as stupid as lending a boy with an increasing habit ten bucks. You don't want to turn him down when he's hurting and you want so much to believe it's not as bad as all that, that he'll be the exception to the junk rule, and that it's still just a kick, even if it is nine in the morning and he's telling you he needs something to take the edge off the day.

*S*he invites me over for brunch. Just you, she says, I only have two plates. She lives on a quiet tree-lined street in the older part of the West Village. She has a backyard. She pays a high rent. She has lived there for three years.

We have only met once before, I am surprised she calls. I want you to see my work, she says, come for brunch. Okay, I say. There is virtually no furniture in her apartment. A table in the middle of the largest of two rooms. Two chairs. She puts the flowers I have brought her in an empty Tropicana bottle and puts it on a corner of the table. This is my portfolio, she says, handing it to me. It's alright. There's one print in it that is really exciting. I tell her so. I don't know what to say about the rest.

She makes scrambled eggs and toast and tea. No coffee. I had wanted coffee. I don't know what I'm doing there. It's not unpleasant. Just uncomfortable. We smoke a joint. We talk about rents and relationships. Of course. We talk about video and painting and parties. Sometimes she doesn't say anything and neither do I. I have to go now, I say later. We should get together again real soon, she says. Yes, I say, I'll call you during the week.

*H*e is thirty-two and his hairline is receding and all he has ever done is play rock'n'roll. In high school, his father said, No, you may not play guitar in a rock'n'roll band. So he developed a pulley system and snuck his guitar out of the second story window after his father had gone to sleep and he went and played guitar in a rock'n'roll band. So there.

He did go to college. He got a degree in engineering. If worse comes to worse, he says, I can go into the studio and produce bands. I know how. He has at various times been a flunky and a roadie and a studio musician, and now he is playing guitar in a moderately popular, well actually a quite popular band. He plays rhythm guitar. I'm not one to take leads, he says. I like staying in the background, he says. But I've seen him play. He didn't stay in the background at all. He was all over the stage. And he looked an awful lot like he enjoyed it too.

*W*e were sitting in one of the back booths in the down-stairs of the club, me on the inside, Brett on the outside, talking about the possibility of my painting a backdrop for the band. The girl, downed-out drunk, falling on her feet, falling out of her low-cut leotard, slid onto the bench, draped her arm around Brett's neck and eased her head onto his shoulder. Hey, baby, the words oozed out of her, I haven't seen you in ages. He made no move to accommodate her. I haven't been around much, he said. Her dark eye make-up was running down her cheeks, her black hair was covering her eyes.

She began to stroke his neck, his face. I kick him under the table. I'm with someone, he says, but does not venture an introduction. She doesn't seem to hear. Perhaps she doesn't care. I've missed you, she says. She will not be shaken off. Perhaps she can't get up. Brett turns his back to her and resumes our conversation. She remains wrapped around him, mumbling in his ear.

Get rid of her, I tell him. It's depressing me.

Look, he says to her, why don't you get lost. He gives her head a boost with his shoulder. She winds herself closer, her face less than an inch from his. Aw, baby, she says, don't be like that.

Brett, I say, I want her out of here.

He, too, has lost patience. He takes his glass and smashes it in half on the table. He holds the jagged bottom half to her face. I shudder. She doesn't. I told you to get away from me, he says. Okay, okay, she says, no reason to be like that, man. She slides off the bench and makes her way to another table.

Brett motions to the waiter. There's been an accident here, he says. Will you get me another drink.

*T*here was a time in the third grade when we all took on boys' names. I wish I were a boy, we all said, I wish I were a boy. I wish I were a boy was the cool thing to say that year.

That same year, a boy named Joshua was in love with me. He told me so. I poured a large jar of blue tempera paint on his head. Moron, I called him. Moron, moron, moron. If you call me moron anymore, he said, I'm going to report you to the principal. So of course, I had to stop.

*C*arrie is addicted to candy corn. She knows each store in the city that stocks it year-round, not just on Halloween. She buys it by the pound. Last month, she bought a bag that contained a large number of burnt kernels in it. Really. She wrote the company. Being as how I am such a great fan of your candy corn, she wrote, I was particularly upset when I recently purchased a bag with burnt kernels in it. She enclosed a sample. White and yellow and orange and black.

When she picked up the box at the post office that came from the candy company, she could hardly control her happiness. It was a big box. At least a month's supply.

It was filled with hard balls.

The nerve, Carrie screams. Just what the hell am I supposed to do with five pounds of hard balls?

*S*leep, baby, sleep.
Thy father tends the sheep.
Thy mother is shaking the dreamland tree,
Shaking down a dream for thee.
Sleep, baby, sleep.

She would climb into bed with me and in her softly confident, off-key voice, she would sing me this song. When I couldn't sleep. Or when I pretended I couldn't, so that I could feel her wrap around me, spoon-like, and sing:

> Sleep, baby, sleep.
> Thy father tends the sheep.
> Thy mother is shaking the dreamland tree,
> Shaking down a dream for thee.
> Sleep, baby, sleep.

She climbed in next to me as she had done so many times. What would the other girls in my class think if they knew? What would the boy in the second row of homeroom think? My mother lying in bed with me and singing a lullaby and me almost thirteen? I can sleep now, I said, squirming from her touch.

Tonight, I wrap my arms about myself and sing it silently to myself.

> Sleep, baby, sleep.
> Thy father tends the sheep.
> Thy mother is shaking the dreamland tree,
> Shaking down a dream for thee.
> Sleep, baby, sleep.

Off-key, too, no doubt.

*H*ey, Sugar. This was his tequila voice. Languorous. Intimate. It was after four a.m.

Where are you, Brett?

The corner of Eleventh and Third. Listen, you wanna elope? We could go to Paris and get married, okay?

Do you want to come over?

Naw, can't Sugar. I gotta go see someone. But tomorrow. Paris. Don't forget. Okay?

He hung up without saying goodnight, as if the receiver had suddenly become too heavy for him to hold onto any longer.

I met Picasso. We were in a crowded room, a party I think, and I was trying to explain to him how very much I admired his work, but I was having difficulty expressing it the way I wanted. I don't suppose, I asked, that you would have time to come and see some of my paintings? I wanted desperately to know what he thought of my work. No, he said, and disintegrated.

*T*he buzzer. Long and plaintive. He would not remove his finger from the button until I was downstairs, in front of him, opening the door.

He walked in and bolted up the stairs and into my apartment. He didn't say hello. He didn't look at me. He walked in rapid circles about the living room, distracted by sounds that only he could hear. His face shone with sweat, his hair was a limp mass of tangles. As he paced, his hand pulled unconsciously at wet knotted strands.

At first, I stood by him, hoping that in one of his rotations he would acknowledge me. Then I moved warily to a chair, scared that any abrupt movement would activate the bomb that was ticking away in rhythm with his steps, his quirks, threatening to explode. I waited.

Every few seconds, he stopped to mutter something unintelligible, looking for my eyes. He bit his lip. He kept on moving. So pale, so taut.

Suddenly, he fell to his knees and heaved deep sobs. I knelt beside him. He seemed a child then, an impenetrable, stricken child.

Have you ever thought of suicide? he asked. Have you ever thought what a rush it would be, sticking that needle in, knowing you were gonna o.d.?

I didn't answer. He didn't expect me to. I held him while he cried.

In a softened, weary voice, he said, I don't know what I would have done if you weren't home. I love you. Come to bed with me.

Afterwards, he took a shower and said he felt just fine.

*O*f course I knew better. I knew better than to think that any amount of moderation is possible with junk. I knew about the line that every junkie crosses when it's no longer a weekend kick, but the very source of life. The point where the drug, the need for it, becomes more important than anything else, including people. When all is rendered an adjunct to the vein. Heroin.

And of course, I refused to see the impact that it was making on Brett, refused to face the fact that his increasingly violent moods weren't due to capriciousness but to his growing single-minded search for something to fill the needle with. The selfishness of the spoon. Heroin. Fucking heroin.

Every now and then, I had noticed a restless, dissatisfied look in his eyes, a film of unabashed hunger. It would wash over his face and flee before I had a chance to study it. But as it began to happen more often, and stay a bit longer, its grasp became harder to ignore. Then he would become lost in it, and as one who is famished has only superficial concentration for anything other than food, he had little for me. It was a possessive, all-encompassing hunger, one that I could do nothing to satisfy. Though of course, I tried.

*P*hil hadn't been around much lately because he had a new girlfriend who no one was exactly wild about. Even Brett, who was usually fascinated by eccentricities, thought this woman was a bit much.

They called her the Kraut. She rarely spoke, at least not to any of us, except when she absolutely had to, and then it was in an unnaturally thick German accent. Her wardrobe leaned heavily towards black leather, with her hair dyed to match. Her eyes were always hidden behind opaque black wrap-around shades.

The truth of the matter, Phil told us the other night in drunken confidentiality, was that her name was Barbara and she lived not far from where she was born, in the Bronx, with her eight year old daughter. He wasn't sure exactly how she supported herself. She remained evasive on that point.

He called a couple of days after that, wanting a female opinion, he said, on their relationship.

It really is getting out of hand, he said. Last night, she fucking punched me in the face for talking to another girl. Can you believe it? She was just an old friend. I don't know what to do about her.

Why don't you stop seeing her, I suggest.

I can't, he says, I'm in love with her.

*T*o be able to become lost in the present, his present. To be able to believe him, believe in his promises as much as he did, as much as I used to. That became my most ardent wish. But my brain could no longer submit, even when the rest of me did.

I had reached a point where intentions no longer satisfied me. Promises no longer held the shadow chance of actuality, but the inevitability of dissolution. I could no longer blindly accept him with the enthusiasm of a fresh convert, but struggled painfully with doubt and cynicism.

Yet still, I made excuses for him with the desperate logic of one who is struggling to maintain a faith that is no longer feasible. Still, I would think, this time he will make good, this time he will not get amnesia. Still, I loved him.

*H*al is fed up with Lisa. You know what she does? he says. She comes and sits in front of the canvas while I'm painting like she's watching television. What am I supposed to do? he asks. She's driving me crazy.

She was out of work for months, he says, but I got real tired of all my money going to feed her instead of to paint so she finally took this job working as a typist in an insurance company. At first she hated it. She couldn't stand the people and she didn't have the right clothes. Now she's borrowed a Sony Walkman from a friend and she listens to the Clash while she types. She says it makes her feel subversive. At least she's paying off her debts.

It's not that I don't love her, Hal says, I do. But I wish she wasn't so fucking dependent on me. Maybe if she had a band ...

What's the matter, Sugar? he asks.

Everything. I say, Can't you see that?

I have no idea what you're talking about.

Listen, Brett, there's always something the matter. Either you've disappeared to god knows where or you're apologizing and swearing you're gonna change or we're euphoric and hiding in bed, but it's always something, Brett, it's never just normal.

Since when were you such a big fan of normal? he asks. It's good between us, better than it's ever been with anyone. You've said that too.

But it's not enough.

What do you want?

Listen, I drink too much when I'm with you, I know that. But lately I've been drinking even more when I'm not with you. Something's wrong. I can't even remember the last time I worked on a painting.

Well, you can't blame that on me.

No, and you can't blame your drugs on me. But it's there.

Sugar, he says, you worry too much. It's good between

us. We love each other. What do you want to go fiddle-fucking around for?

*H*e grabbed the mike stand and tilted it towards him. Listen, he growled, the party's at her house. He nodded in my direction and gave my address. You're all invited, he said. I had no voice. He looked down at me, not laughing, but smiling triumphantly, as I shook my head, no, no, no. There was laughter in the audience. They were, after all, being let in on something, was it an inside joke? was it really a party? were they really being invited to a party? He had made his point, whatever that was. He took pity on me. Or he simply lost interest. Anyway, he said, Sorry, folks, but it looks like the party's been cancelled. Lack of ice. Next time.

*H*er parents are like this. Once they were broke. I guess even people with big houses can sometimes be broke. Any-way, they were broke and her father didn't tell her mother they were broke. They didn't discuss finances, that was his department, so he didn't tell her they were broke. He didn't want to worry her.

So she went on about her way, buying designer clothes and new gadgets for the kitchen and presents for her hus-band and children and giving money to charity and the like. How was she to know they were broke. He took out loans.

And then business picked up. He was even able to open a new store. And then another one. They had plenty of money now. His wife still didn't know that they ever hadn't.

One day, Carrie overheard her father on the phone. He made reference to the time they were broke. I never thought we'd make it, he said. She asked her mother. Mom, she said, why didn't you ever tell me we were once broke? What? her mother said, where did you ever get such an idea?

*L*eather pants look stupid in summer and I really don't care anymore who is playing where and I am sick of these club bathrooms with the paper always on the floor and I am sick of hanging out waiting for you after your gigs while you run off to chat up some lady reporter, and I am tired of your friends, checking veins, checking brains, seeing who's got anything left, and what the price is.

*T*he overgrown children who still protested bedtime, the drunk, the doped-up, the hangers-on, the hangers-out, the young, the hip, the insomniacs, trying to make the night, the party, last forever. Dancing, dealing, falling on each other, falling away from each other, laughing, sneering, playing pinball, nodding out in corners, yelling over the latest hit tunes, whispering, mumbling, silent. At six a.m., the club was just hitting its stride.

We were seated against the back wall, not talking, glad for the ongoing distraction from each other, and from the dawn that was sure to be lurking just outside of the club's mottled walls, threatening to illuminate the night's hungover complexion. Like homesick tourists, we were silent observers of the activity swirling around us, joined by our mutual desire to avoid the daylight. It came as an unwelcome intrusion, a forgery. We were unprepared for it.

He spoke first. I've been with so many other women, he said, I wouldn't even recognize most of their eyes. He was offering an absent reflection, not a threat, it was too late for that, and I was not jealous of his other women, not anymore, only of his ability to forget.

And mine? I asked.

I knew that he wished he could erase mine the way he had the others, and I knew too that he would never be able to, and that was what was disturbing him.

No, he said, looking up at me as if to make sure, no.

We were again silent for a while, both looking out into the room as if watching a parade of images on television without bothering to follow the story. It was beginning to make me dizzy, the smoke that lingered at eye level, weaving its odor through our hair like a seductress, the waltz of the coupling and uncoupling, the music that had ceased to be songs, but functioned as the only acceptable soundtrack to keep the action moving.

I excused myself and went to the bathroom. Men and women, passing out, passing drugs, passing hot tips and cold gossip. I had had enough. I had had more than enough.

I'm tired, I said as I resumed my seat.

All I wanted was to leave. He lit a fresh cigarette. He was still thinking about us, still trying to make some kind of sense of it.

You know the dark side, he said, as if bestowing me with a medal. That's why I stay with you, you understand.

Don't you see, I wanted to say, I don't want to understand. I don't want your dark side. I was only supposed to be a visitor, maybe lead you away, I don't know, but I certainly had no intentions of staying. Take away my understanding, I wanted to say, drown it, kill it, shoot it full of morphine, but take it back. Please, please, take away my medals and give me back my civilian clothes, I've had enough, I wanted to say. But I didn't have the energy.

I'm tired, I said, I just want to go home. Stay if you want to.

Can't you wait til I finish my drink?

No.

Goodnight then.

Goodnight.

*O*nce, we were at a football game and it was freezing cold. My feet are so cold they're numb, I said. Take off your boots and I'll rub them, he said. I took off my boots and put my feet in his lap. He rubbed them. Better? he asked after a while. Yes, I said. I put my boots back on. I kissed him. Thank you.

It's hard to imagine in this heat wave having numb feet. It's also hard to imagine being nineteen and at a football game.

*L*arry called this morning with some advice about my artistic career. You must remember two things, he said, if you are serious about becoming a success. It's who you know and who you blow.

—

*D*on't be ridiculous, Carrie says. There's no need to fuck anybody. I mean, why not just beg? It's cleaner. Groveling is good too, Carrie says.

I can't go on like this. I just can't. It doesn't make any sense, no sense at all.

There must have been a reason someplace along the line, there must have been. But I'll be goddamned if I can remember what the hell it was.

I can't even remember where I was supposed to end up.

*S*o listen, Rimbaud was wrong. The foolish virgin does eventually get hip to the infernal bridegroom. She does eventually come out of delirium. Yes. Of course.

You're not gonna take me down with you. You think you can, but you can't. Not this time, uh uh. I'm not coming with you. You think I am, but I'm not. Go find yourself another Persephone. I'm not gonna keep house in your hell. Uh uh.

No yo-yo this time, baby, ain't gonna be your goddam yo-yo. Up, down, round the world, into the palm of your hand. Gonna break the string and leave you with a rotting umbilical cord. Junkies' babies are hooked at birth, but I'm kicking, lover, I'm kicking.

Don't it just leave you with a knot in your stomach?

*I*t could happen again. Don't ever forget that. It could happen again. That was pretty much the extent of my re-

ligious upbringing, except for one or two cousins' bar mitz-
vahs, and presents on or about the first day of Chanukah,
whenever was most convenient.

But it could happen again. That was drilled into me. Don't
ever forget. Don't ever forget. It could happen again.

*P*ainful—because it's true. And indisputable. A fact. It's
over. And because it hurts—like a knife held against your
throat. You know that feeling? Like a knife cold hard mean
against your throat and you just wanna say—kill me, I don't
care, fuck me, I don't care. And you don't.

But then again, you do. You care more than anything, and
you're conscious of that caring like a new cut, but you're
too fucking frozen terrified to say a word. Maybe you don't
care so much after all.

We were diametrically opposed, but precisely the same.
Though we would never admit it, never. It was too dangerous.

Over, over.

*S*he married a man stupider than her. Not a stupid man.
But stupider than her.

A kind man, a gentle and attentive and attractive man. A
man who idolizes her, like her father idolizes her mother.
In other days, he would have been called a simple man. She
is happy with him. You could see it coming.

It was a big church wedding. Lace and priests and all. A
real wedding. They joked about it, of course, but you could
see it coming.

They will not add to the divorce rate. They will have children soon and a house. They will be happy. You can see it coming.

I have a retarded brother, Hal says. Something told me not to laugh and say, Well, you should see my sister. Thank god.

He's thirty now, he says. He lives at home. My mother takes care of him. Sometimes he sweeps up at the local hardware store. It's important for him to have a sense of money. He buys food with it. Brownies and Oreos mostly. He used to keep them stashed in his room, but it was attracting too many bugs, so Mother convinced him to keep them in the refrigerator. He said okay as long as his name was written on them so everyone would know they were his and not theirs. She tags everything, Hal says.

I hope you're not being promiscuous, she said. Promiscuous. Promiscuity. A mother's word, if ever there was one. Promiscuous. I'm still not sure what it means.

Things my mother told me about sex. That's the point here.

Before I went off to college, she told me this. She said, Don't come home after your first semester and tell me you've already been to the birth control center. Yes, Mother, I said. I did not, of course, tell her that it was already too late.

Then once, while I was home on vacation, she came into

my bedroom and sat down on my bed and lit a cigarette and said, This woman at the club today told me that she has never had an orgasm. Can you believe that? They had all been reading the latest best seller on female sexuality. And you? I asked. You know I can't talk about things like that, she said.

What else. She said this once. She said, Don't think I don't know the guilt of sleeping with someone you shouldn't be sleeping with, because I do. And I said, What? And she walked away.

Last week, she called me up and said, I hope you are not on the pill, especially with the amount you smoke, they say it is very bad for you. And I said, Yes, I know. And she said, I do not mean for you to think that I am in any way condoning promiscuity. I do not expect you to be promiscuous. And I said, Yes, I know.

*H*e wore a tan well-cut suit and a white shirt open at the neck. He had a mild suntan, a Cartier watch, a leather shoulder bag. He had stylishly cut light brown hair. We had been talking about lofts and the like. Would you like to go for a drink? he asked. Okay, I said.

We were in Soho. We went to a chic Soho bar. When the waitress came to take our order, I said to her, I'll have a vodka on the rocks. He ordered a vodka and grapefruit juice. I have to make a phone call, I say to him. When I come back, the waitress is putting the drinks on the table. In front of me, she places a water glass filled to the brim. It is all vodka. I didn't order that, I say to her. She looks embarrassed. I know, she says, he ordered it for you. She walks away. I am capable of ordering my own drinks, I say to him, and I'm not going to sleep with you. I'm sorry, he says.

We move on to other topics. His career. He buys lofts and renovates them and sells them. I am somewhat interested. I tell him that I am a painter and that painters need lofts for painting. We talk more about his career. He does not ask about mine. For all he knew, or cared, I could be illustrating comic books.

He reaches for my hand across the table. He wants to fondle it and look into my eyes. What are you doing? I ask him. I can't understand why he would want to fondle my hand and look into my eyes. Why don't you trust me? he asks. I feel as if I am playing by a different set of rules. I feel single. For the first time in my life, I feel single. A Single. The kind that there are news specials about. The Singles Lifestyle.

I'm going home now, I say to him. Okay, he says, and signs for the drinks. Can I take you home? he asks. No thank you, I say.

*H*al is laughing. I was just thinking, he says. Last night, I found a fresh piece of bubble gum stuck on the wood sculpture I'm working on. You could still smell the grape. I asked Lisa about it. You know what she said? She said it was in the way. She was so fucking nonchalant I couldn't even get angry.

*T*here was no one to call and there was nothing on television and there was nothing to do and it was Sunday.

I had already read the paper and I had already had breakfast and I had run out of cash and there was nothing I really would have wanted to spend it on anyway. And it was still only one o'clock and I couldn't face painting cause I had messed up the canvas I was working on yesterday and I wasn't ready to prime a new one and I could have gone for a walk, but I didn't much feel like getting dressed. All I could do was miss him. Yes. I did miss him.

I felt the energy and desire to paint, I felt the need, I most certainly felt that, but the flow was not there. In my absence from it, I had lost my sense of rhythm. The images that materialized on canvas were out of step with those I visualized.

Just a matter of time, I thought, just a matter of time. Right?

*I*f only I had been a little cooler ...
If only I had tried harder to get him to kick ...
If only I had been more affectionate ...
If only I had been more demanding ...
If only I hadn't gotten involved to begin with ...
If only I had been prettier ...
If only I had been a better lover ...
If only I had yelled more ...
If only I had had more patience ...
If only I had been more insistent ...
If only I had been more understanding ...

It was gonna be like Paris / **105**

If only I hadn't cared so much . . .
If only I had known . . .
If only . . .
If only . . .
If only . . .

*G*irls' night out, Carrie says. Forget your troubles, c'mon get happy. I don't feel like going out, I say. Shut up and get dressed, she says. We're gonna dance all your blues away.

Two Piña Coladas, Carrie tells the waiter. Stop looking so fucking gloomy, she tells me. Two more, Carrie tells the waiter as he puts down the first round, we have a depressed girl here. Here, she says, slipping an oblong package bedecked with purple curly ribbons and silver glitter out of her bag. It is a paint brush. Get it dirty, she says, and don't call me until you do.

We have two more. At least. Carrie talks a lot. She is not particularly interested in anything I have to say, unless it has nothing to do with Brett and nothing I have to say tonight will have nothing to do with Brett. All Carrie will say to that is, Good riddance. Anyway, despite my best efforts, I somehow have an awfully good time.

Later, we are skipping down the street. Yes. Skipping. Carrie is half a block ahead of me when I see her jump into a garbage can. I start running and tripping and laughing and screaming. What the hell are you doing? Her arms and legs are sticking straight up. Well, Carrie says, I've lived in this neighborhood long enough, don't you think it's time I experienced it from the bums' perspective? We are both laughing hard and crying. Get me out of here, she says when she catches her breath. I start yanking her arms, but she will not budge. I can't, I say. What do you mean, you can't? I pull at various combinations of hands and feet, but we are both too hysterical to be effective. Carrie begins to panic. What are we going to do? Her voice is trembling. Don't worry, I say, I'll go get help. Just hold on, she says, you don't think you're leaving me alone like this, do you? We see a man coming towards us. He helps to tip the garbage can and get Carrie out.

I like this, she says as we are once again making our way down the street, you break up with your boyfriend and I'm the one who ends up in a heap.

*H*e showed up again. Of course he did.

He came over to where I was sitting and wrapped his arms around me. I did not protest and I did not respond. I could do neither. Maybe, maybe it would be okay, maybe we could forget, maybe, just for tonight, maybe, maybe . . .

Why are you here? I asked.

I just felt like being with you, he said, isn't that enough?

And then you won't feel like being with me and you'll just disappear?

Can't we just be together for tonight and not worry about it? he asked.

What do you think? Do you think that if you get me to go to bed with you, we'll be back where we started from. I'm supposed to forget everything?

What do you want from me? He was annoyed. Why did I have to go and open my mouth and ruin everything. What the fuck do you want from me? You know I'm sorry, I've already told you that. You want to give me thirty lashes? Go ahead. You want to chain me up and make me beg forgiveness?

Don't be stupid.

You're crazy, he said. You know that? You are fucking crazy! He started for the door.

And you're walking out again. That's what you always do, one way or another, as soon as there's a little trouble, you walk out.

You're crazy. You know what your problem is? Your problem is that you don't know what you want. You're crazy.

I know what I want. I want an explanation. I don't want any more of your goddam apologies. I'm tired of those. I just want an explanation. I just want to understand. Make me understand.

He didn't hear. He was already down the stairs, still yelling, you're crazy, you're fucking crazy, you're crazy.

*V*aliums. Valiums to sleep. Valiums to wake. Valiums to walk. Blue. Yellow. Whatever. One with coffee. One with a Tab. One with a martini. Don't worry, they said, we'll bring you some valiums. Just enough to make it through this week. After that, it will be easier. It's got to get easier.

One gives you a light buzz. Just enough to relax and re-enact you. Enough to make you want another. And if you're lucky, you will have a little distance with two. Not that the pain goes away, no, but it separates enough so that you can look at it, coddle it, and if you take another, decide that you will stash it for another day. Three or four or more.

No more.

Somewhere along the way, the progression backfires. Two plus two does not equal four. The numbness is no longer a refuge, but a tingling cage that you cannot fight your way out of. And as the difference between sleeping and waking blurs, it seems that you have done neither in, how long? that you have been hanging in a hellish limbo where actions are only futile gestures and emotions have been diffused into an incessantly threatening mass with no definition.

No more.

*B*lake was a smart old cat. With his hallucinations and illusions and all. And no one knew if they were real or not. No one knew. Aw, c'mon, some of them said, cut the crap, Blake. And some of them said, My, my, there goes one illuminated dude. Yessiree. And no one knew. Maybe old Blake didn't either. But what drawings, what drawings.

*W*aiting for Patty. Patty is late and I am hungry. The waitress is eyeing me as are some of the customers, looking at me look for Patty. Are they looking at me with that knowing look with which they look at women who are in the process of being stood up? Are they?

Patty comes flinging in. I'm sorry I'm late, she says, but I was getting laid. I figured you'd understand.

*C*arrie says I don't need a shrink. She says she has a sure-fire cure for insecurities of any kind. She says I should just go out and get myself a leather jacket. She says it will do more for my attitude than any shrink could in years and be cheaper in the long run. That's what Carrie says.

*H*e said he liked my paintings and I believed him. He seemed too drunk to lie. He stood there for so long, analyzing them, reading into them what he would—Christ, he was so obvious, it was boring, but he was there, and he wasn't about to leave, and just a few hours ago, I had wanted him there, so I supposed it was okay. But I wished we could just go to bed already. I wished he would leave my paintings out of it, they had absolutely nothing to do with why he was there. Nothing. But that would have been rude to point out.

He was looking for a friend, he was looking for a lover, he was looking for a Relationship. He was sincere, my god, he was even sweet. I wished we could just go to bed already, I had had enough talk. I mean, if that was what I wanted, I certainly wouldn't have wasted my time with him. I did not want a critic. I did not want a boyfriend. All I wanted was to go to bed with him. All I wanted was to see what it was like not to care.

I couldn't wait for him to leave the next morning. I wanted to get on with things. I wanted to get to work. He had nothing to do with anything.

*W*e had already had our last time together. That was out of the way. So when we ran into each other in the club, and we talked to each other, sometimes we didn't, but this time we did, we talked and we touched each other, we knew it would not be the last time because we had already had that.

Let me take you home, he said.

I don't know, I said. I didn't know, but god, did I want to be convinced. He kissed me hard and deep and I was flooded with yes, yes, of course, yes.

We made love for hours, for ever. We did not sleep. You see, he said, we could still make it work. We could live together. I'll change, really, I won't get so fucked up, and you could still have your room for painting. We should live together. I wouldn't care if you wanted other lovers from time to time, but we should be together.

It wouldn't work, I said. I kissed him. Calmly. I did not need his permission to take other lovers. I did not need his permission to paint. We could never make it work, I said, not in real life.

Well then, he said, we could have an affair that lasts for-ever, we should always be lovers, despite our real lives. Lovers without expectations.

We could never be lovers without expectations, I said.

I love you, he said. Of course. Of course I loved him too. I knew that. But it no longer mattered.

*T*his is an ad that appeared in the paper.

benefits in exchange for lease on Manhattan apt. Good size apt. for minimum rent. Marriage for apt. benefits exchange only!

And then a box number.

*E*rrol and his dogs. Again. He took Wellington for a walk early this morning, about seven a.m., forgetting to bring a scooper or a piece of paper with him. One can't remember everything at that hour, darling, especially where I was coming from.

Well, when Wellington took a crap—three times around the block, that animal can be so stubborn sometimes!—on the sidewalk, Errol started to cross the street to get a piece of paper out of the trash can when he was assaulted by a fellow dog-walker, an aging faggot he knew, who accused him of being the cause of decay of New York's streets. How can you just walk away from this mess? he screeched. Have you no breeding?

Honey, Errol replied, I have more breeding in my left pinky than you and your dog put together.

I just hate middle-aged queens with paunches, he said, don't you? Especially when they're not exactly loose with the cash.

His hair, Errol's that is, is an orange crew cut this week. And he dyed his body hair to match.

Pubic hair too? I ask.

Well of course, darling.

*I*t's always the same when I'm drunk. A cubistic distortion. The right eye inches lower than the left, sliding into the cheek, the mouth dipping and rising assymetrically, the hairline a warp of scallops.

Sometimes I can stare into the mirror endlessly, curious, fascinated. It isn't me, after all. And sometimes it repulses and frightens me, and the relation between this disaster and myself is blurred, confusing.

*T*his is what she does. She comes home from work and brings the portable television into the bathroom and watches the news while she lies in a bubble bath in the dark. She is a writer. In her room, there are two framed pictures. One is of Lou Reed. The other is of William Butler Yeats. She says she is working on a novel. Sometimes, she spends the afternoon in bed, watching soap operas and scribbling in her notebooks. It's almost done, she says. She has been saying that for quite some time.

*P*ushing, pulling, pushing, pulling, remembering when. Remember when? Does he ever remember when?

Remembering when, thinking if only, wondering if. Does he ever wonder if?

Remembering when . . .

Christ, you'd think I'd know better by now than to believe in the Phoenix.

*H*e walked in purposefully. A good sign, I thought. He'll pick up his things and go. No nonsense. He even had a friend in tow, a stand-up comic, at least by ambition. Hi, Sugar, he kissed me on the cheek, as if he was just getting home from the office and I had his drink waiting for him. You want some juice? he asked his friend. There isn't any, I said.

Your clothes are over there, I said, in those bags. Yeah, he shrugged his shoulders, I'll get them later. A minor detail. He went into the bathroom and shot up and came out and picked up the paper. Just like old times.

Your clothes, I reminded him as he got ready to leave.

I'm on my way to rehearsal, he said, and I don't feel like carrying them around with me. You don't mind if I come back later to pick them up, do you?

I started to nod. Out of habit. But I stopped. Yes, I said, I do mind. Take them now or I'll throw them out.

What's the big deal? He seemed genuinely baffled.

Take them now.

He looked at his friend. Women.

Okay, he said as if humoring a mental patient, okay.

*L*arry has been seeing someone besides his steady boyfriend lately. A young boy, and none too bright either, from what Larry says. It's a private matter, he doesn't go out with him, he doesn't introduce him.

Dumb, he says, completely illiterate, but god can he fuck.

Bring him to the opening, I suggest.

Are you kidding, he says, I wouldn't bring him to the opening of an envelope.

*N*ick leaning over the counter, his golden tanned shoulderblades lunging out of his white ribbed T-shirt, reading the paper, leaning over the counter with his sort-of-blond hair slicked back and his defiant cheekbones making waves and his hands beating out restless rhythms, too cool to turn to you, too cool to turn to, but yes, you want to, god yes, you want to, even though you know better, know better from Brett, from all the trouble boys, but because you know, you think, It will be different this time, this time it will be different.

That's what you're thinking, anyway, that's what you thought, when you first looked at each other, looked at each other with recognition and wariness and taunt, no need for introductions here, we already know each other.

And you can't touch him and he won't touch you and it won't be different this time, no different at all, you know that he is the same, and you don't want it, no, but maybe since you know ... so you think, who will give first? huh? who will give first?

And then the next day, you think better of the whole thing, which is, it turns out, just as well, for he has disappeared.

I would like to learn sparsity. I would like to make cool, clean canvases with cool clean pastel colors, middle grays and salmons, with cool clean shapes, self-contained shapes that stick to their business and do not interfere with each other. But of course, I don't.

I got a great rejection letter today, she said. She was not being sarcastic. I had thought at first that she might be, but she wasn't. They said they wanted to see some more of my work in a couple of months. Isn't that wonderful? she said. Wonderful, I said.

*J*effrey used to want to make films. He went to school and he studied film-making and he went to the movies and he read magazines and books and he talked about making films. And then he came to New York and he got a job fixing cameras and he didn't talk so much anymore about making films except for every now and then when he would meet some director or another who he particularly admired and then he would get excited, but that didn't happen very often. His job was drudgery. He applied to the union, but he wasn't very excited.

He quit his job. I still like going to the movies, he says, but I can't stand the business side. I'm going to do something else. He doesn't know what yet. Maybe something in real estate. There comes a time, he says, when you wake up and realize something is just a hobby. Don't you think?

*T*erry has no water in his building. The building is on a rent strike. The landlord is trying to force them out of their cheap lofts and make them into expensive lofts. There is little to stop him.

Terry came over for buckets of water. He takes the oldest child to the gas station across the street to use the bathroom. Luckily, he says, the youngest is still in diapers. I'm not so sure, he says, whether I want to raise my children here after all.

*W*e had been introduced. A friend of a friend. Or a sort of friend of a sort of friend. It was late. No one was taking responsibility.

You like pinball? he asks.

Yeah, I say, thinking the game would lessen the need for conversation.

Me too, he says. You know why?

Why?

Because it's visual, he says, like foreplay. I like foreplay too. And you know what? he asks. I'm good at both. I know how to play those flippers, he says.

That's nice, I say.

You live alone? he asks.

Absolutely not, I say.

*O*n your hands. Or on paper. But never, never sit on a public toilet. You just never know. No sense in taking chances. Never sit on the seat, dear.

And of course, I don't.

*D*on't break skin. Don't stay up. Don't do anything ir-revocable. Most of all, don't do that. Don't, don't, don't do anything irrevocable. Be cool and distanced and right and fitting. Don't do anything irrevocable. There must be no scars.

Have a dance. Celebrate. Paint your toes. Dance, dance, dance.

*S*orry, folks, but you'll have to sit up front, this station's closed. The waitress is in the bathroom trying to get off on two-bit burning heroin that the Puerto Rican busboy gave her cause she's been so down lately. The Puerto Rican busboy got it off his dealing lover who cuts her coke with too much lactose and calls him at his wife's in the middle of the night. The Puerto Rican busboy works seven nights a week and is generous with his drugs, the minuscule foils that he slips in pockets, but no one even wants them anymore cause his drugs are shit. The waitress, though, says thank-you this time anyway, and slips it in her apron, sticky with spilt syrup, grabs a straw and goes into the bathroom where she opens the foil clumsily and spills the powder onto the scuffed black toilet seat, feeling what little high there is wrap around her dragging brain. She flushes her nostrils out with water and goes out to take orders.

*M*ore wine? Yes, yes, I'll get you both some more wine. A new album. Faster. No, the next song is better. Faster. Drink, drink. Laugh. Faster. Stay. Here, I'll dress up for you—hats, scarves. I'll paint my face. I'll make you laugh. Just stay. Cigarette. Another cigarette. Faster, louder. Talk to me. Anything will do. Faster, though, faster. Tell me a story. No pauses, please, no silence. Here, this is my gypsy look. Do you like my eyes? Have you seen this new book? This new print? Yes, yes, I know you've been here before, but I'm sure there are things that you haven't seen. More wine? Don't yawn. Maybe I have some speed you can take. Don't yawn. Stay. Faster. Drink, talk, stay. We need loud rock'n'roll. Stay. Another butt. Fast. Fast. Faster.

No loneliness tonight. All is shining and fine and I can make it. Faster. Shall we go out? The bar down the street. Let's run and sing and be happy tonight. Yes, I'm fine, wonderful, but it's so fucking cluttered in here—butts and glasses and costumes and dirt. I can't stand it. We must leave right away. Let's go now. Fast. C'mon, we've got to get out of here. Fast. It is filthy, rancid. Clutter. Quickly, quickly. We are almost there.

No, no, I don't want a drink. Don't ask me. Don't ask me anything. No words. I can't breathe in here. Out. Air. I'm okay, really. I just have to relax a little, that's all. It's the street lights quivering, the cars, the faces, wide-angled clutter.

I'm going home. I'm going to become a hermit. No drugs, no lovers, no friends, no words. It's all clutter. I'll get rid of it all—soiled canvases and ashtrays. Too much clutter. I'll throw it all away.

It's still so dirty in here. So cluttered. No more. All I want is emptiness. I'm okay. Really. You can leave now. Leave now, please leave. You are clutter too.

I have invented a new art form, he says. He has a beard. He is a graduate student from Philadelphia. There's some convention here for graduate students in art history. They're everywhere. A shopping expedition, he says.

I call it solo art, he says. It's all a matter of perception, completely cerebral. Someone bumps into me on the way to the bar. For example, he continues, let's say that I come across a certain angle that coincides with an angle that I have previously imagined. Then that is it. That's what? I ask. Art, he says. And then what? I ask. Then nothing, he says. Oh, I suppose you can attempt to verbalize it for the benefit of others, but that's not quite the point. What do you do? he asks.

*I*t comes back. I am not ready to leave it behind. I may be drunk. And tired. But it comes back. I will not give it up. Not now.

I can paint with rock'n'roll and cigarettes. I can have a throat that burns from assault and a mind that somersaults with weariness. But it comes back. I can feel it. I can paint. I can feel it.

*T*his. Quicksilver, shaky, sharp thin. A thin that clearly stems from nerves, not dieting. Thinness that constantly chills, that calls for an ever-present cardigan for protection.

A virgin at thirty-two, she shies from your touch as if from a leper. If by chance you bump into her, even slightly brush her arm, she bolts and glares and sulks until her skin has forgotten the impression that has been forced upon it, her ivory skin that barely washes over the sky-blue veins.

She wears bright red lipstick, carefully applied with a brush. She studies tarot and astrology. She spent seven years in analysis. It didn't help, she says. She still holds only her cats. She still thinks of death each night. Once, she took a hundred valiums. And called her psychiatrist before they took effect. They pumped her stomach. They added another year or two on to her treatment. Now she owes them six thousand dollars.

We are on our third cup of coffee. We are talking about knitting. Orlon versus cotton versus wool.

I wish I were dead, she says. A simple statement of fact. We go back to our small talk.

I wish I were dead, she says again a few minutes later. Oh, I guess I said that already, she adds, suddenly embarrassed for herself.

*L*arry is talking about his childhood. I always used to change things, he says. I always thought I could make them better. My mother would buy me a pair of pants and I would say, They're nice, but I can make them better. And I would. She would buy me a pair of shoes, and I would cut them up into sandals. Once, he says, she hid all the scissors in the house for two months. But I found other ways.

*I*t's so restful in here. One a.m. Sitting by candlelight. Drinking wine. The only voices are from the outside. They are not about me.

The canvas turned out well. Real well. The expression is perfect, just how I wanted it. She looks right at you, right at you.

▬▬▬

*W*e talked. We talked about museums and painting and growing up. We talked about the unemployment rate and sex on television. We compared neighborhoods and brands of cigarettes. We compared past lovers. I offered him a sketch of Brett. What did you ever think you could gain from that relationship? he asked. I guess I didn't think about that, I said. He didn't understand. And you? I asked. I have a history, he said, knocking the ice about in his drink, of getting involved with messed-up women. Messed-up? I asked. I didn't understand. Messed-up, he said. The kind that it is impossible to carry on a relationship with. And we talked about going to the beach and books and composers.

I think I should get going, I said. It was after two.

Okay, he said, I'll walk you to a cab. He reached for his sneakers. He walked me to a cab. He didn't kiss me good-night. We had had a lovely evening. Talking. Gary.

I have at times doubted it. I have even at times tried denying it. I have ignored and belittled it, tried wishing it away, wishing away the need. I have even come close to succeeding.

But I know, I know more than I know anything else, that it is indeed crucial to me. And it always will be.

Back to work.

*C*arrie looks at her arm. The scars, once carefully etched in by a razor blade, are beginning to fade. I had hoped they wouldn't, Carrie says. I've gotten used to them, their sickly purple carbon copy reminder.

I can't imagine meeting someone a few years from now, she says, completely clean, unlined. I can't imagine the scars completely faded and the cuts just an anecdote that I might choose to tell, or not. I can't imagine, she says, not having the evidence.

*H*e goes to work every day. He wakes up every morning and goes to work. It's been a long time since I've known anyone who does that. Who goes to work every day. Not for a week or two, when you're broke, but for, well, for ever. But he has this career—in advertising. He's a junior executive, or something like that. And he likes it too. He goes to work every day and he likes it. Really.

*S*itting on the stoop with Sam at dusk, summer dusk, when people begin to emerge, to stroll and meander in the subsiding heat. Couples. Couples. They all seem to be couples.

Sam is talking about his girlfriend. Which is rare for him. He prefers to keep her hidden. Away from his working companions. Away from his day-to-day conversation. He has been seeing her for six years. Not six solid years, he is quick to point out. Nevertheless, he has been seeing her, on and off, for six years.

They are about to enter one of their off periods. She doesn't want to be my girlfriend, he says.

Why not? I ask.

For the same reason that I didn't used to want to be her boyfriend. For the same reason that no one ever wants to be anyone's boyfriend or girlfriend, he says, though he doesn't tell me what that reason is.

A free jazz concert at eight on a pier near the tip of Manhattan. Sitting on the wooden planks alongside the majestic rise of the old black, white and yellow ship that presides over the sky, the concert. A white, New York, jazz audience, beards, shapeless dresses, babies, blankets and wine, ageless.

During his string of announcements and introductions, the announcer says that there is to be no smoking on the pier. The audience erupts into elated claps and yelps. The trio comes onstage. They play, by and large, the cocktail variety of jazz, lounge music, mood music, perfect for the deepening blue sky, the occasional neon flash of an ascending plane, the fish funk smell of the East River.

I spill some wine on Gary's foot. We laugh. We talk in lowered voices, not quite whispers, we are outside, after all. A woman comes and leans over us. She has a crew cut, large tortoise-shell glasses and sagging breasts. Some of us are trying to listen to the music, she says in a nasal tone. We look up at her, the librarian who singled us out in the second grade, the teacher who intercepted our notes. She looks down at us with arched eyebrows. Irreverent people have no business at a jazz concert. She straightens her back and walks away.

We enjoy ourselves anyway. It's dark when the concert ends. We have finished the wine. We walk a ways before catching the bus home.

*H*e lifted up the back of his T-shirt to show me. Across the left side of his back was a cracking crimson semi-circle.

I was working on the lower part of my painting, Hal says, and I was crouched in the same position on the ladder for over an hour. When I went to stand up, I saw all these incredible colors. It was really cool. I knew what was happening, but the colors were so great, I kept on getting up. Next thing I know, I'm flat out on the floor. When I felt the pain in my back, I thought I had a heart attack or something. That's the first time I ever fainted, Hal says.

I can't remember a single time when he actually said, I love you. Not once. I never really thought about it growing up, it didn't occur to me that he didn't, so I just didn't think about it. But looking back, I wish he had told me occasionally. I still wish he would.

*S*he plays drums. She's only twenty-seven, but she looks older. She is from Tennessee. She has a Tennessee drawl. I came up here to have fun, she says, and when I'm finished having fun, then I'm goin' back home.

She might be delicate, but she isn't. She plays drums. She

plays with a band that's just forming. They're real good, she says.

She has a tattoo on her right forearm. It's not a real tattoo, someone did it at a party she was at a couple of nights ago. You rub on the outline, she explains, and then paint it in with these special paints. The girl who did it is real good. Y'all should have seen it a couple of days ago, it was real beautiful.

I like it anyway. It is a bird, I don't know what kind, with its wings spread. Gold, amber, paling red, leaking over a black border. I wish I had seen it a couple of days ago.

I can hone it all down. I can make it simple, clear. I can take out all of the details, all of the details that are cluttering them up. I can make them good.

*A*t first, he was like familiar terrain, with no new language to learn, no new climate to become accustomed to. And like one returning home after a long stay in a foreign land, I noted a few new developments, but thought, well, it is essentially the same place after all. I was, of course, aware of the changes I had gone through, the new tastes and new standards, the new prejudices, and I wanted to make them as clear to him as they were to me. But really, it was good to be home. It was reassuring. Wasn't it?

*H*e worked at a manic pace, pouring paint on six-by-eight canvases. He had to finish fifty-three of them in nine days. He had to. He owed the gallery.

He hired me to mix the paints. Gallons and gallons and gallons of paint, scarlets, grays, peaches. At first, I could only think of what the paint cost. A dribble here, a drop there, what if I blew it? And then I became wildly cavalier, Oh ho ho, a bucket of this, a bucket of that, what the hell. It wasn't my money after all.

For the last three days, he let me hire an assistant. The pressure to finish was strong. I let my assistant clean the brushes, sweep the floors, scrub. I just mixed.

*M*y first dance was the Junior High School Christmas Dance. My mother brought home five velvet dresses from Saks for me to choose from. I set my hair. I was allowed to wear lipstick. I danced. I don't remember what shoes I wore. I don't remember who I danced with. But I remember how it felt. The heavy black velvet and the high lace neck and the boys' legs pushing into mine and their hands moist and heavy on my back. Slow dancing, stationary dancing. Twelve inches, the Headmaster said as he patrolled the clinging couples with a ruler. Twelve inches. You must remain twelve inches apart. Standing in the center of the floor hugging does not constitute dancing, he said. This is a dance.

At the Christmas Dance the next year, none of us wore velvet and none of us set our hair and certainly none of us wore lipstick. We wore blue jeans, hopefully with rips and patches, and we did not touch when we danced. That year, the Headmaster and the chaperones patrolled the bathrooms and the corridors, following the thick smell of marijuana.

*W*e were busy being awkwardly affectionate and I was putting off getting dressed and on my way for as long as possible. It was our first morning after our first night together and I didn't care if I was a little late for work.

He lay with his hands under his head, watching me buckle the ankle straps of my sandals. There was no time for coffee, there was no need for him to get up. I leaned over and kissed him goodbye. I'll see myself out, I said.

As I was opening the door, I heard him behind me. Here, he said, naked as could be, holding out a five-dollar bill. The least I can do is pay for your cab.

I looked at him for a minute, wondering about etiquette and the earnest smile on his face. No thanks, I said, I can pay for my own transportation.

*T*his girl I know went to North Carolina with John the Baptist, a Hell's Angel. They made it in fourteen hours, even though the tank of his Harley didn't hold much gas and they had had to stop frequently. There was going to be a big run there, about five hundred Angels. Before they left, she said to John, No sharing me, okay? No gang bangs. She had heard about Angels. No, he said, just say you're with me. She tried not to let him out of her sight. She met another girl down there with a broken nose. She had refused to give an Angel head. He punched her and then he and his buddies raped her. On Tuesday afternoon, John the Baptist discovered that he was holding hands with this girl that he had taken to North Carolina with him. He pushed her away. You're ruining my image, he said. She took the Greyhound back.

*H*ow strange, to suddenly be walking on the beach, sitting on the rocks by the jetty, picking up shells, watching the children with their bright pails and their slipping suits, and the blues, those must be the blues that held painters in the south of France, those magnificent blues and the piercing keenness of the light and lines and the rhythmic lapping, not at all busy. Stepping out, stepping out. A day at the beach, tarred feet and freckles, and they serve beer on the train back and by nine o'clock we are tanned and tired and in bed, still feeling the waves and seeing the blues.

*D*eirdre wants me to pass judgment. Deirdre has an acute political awareness. It is not any one thing that Deirdre wants me to pass judgment on, but everything, everyone. Everything is, after all, political. Everything has implications. How can you not see that? she asks. She is frustrated with me. I know she is. I am frustrated with her. I wonder if she knows. I cannot say, So what? to her, because, after all, she is right, isn't she? So I say, I'm tired of talking. Then do something, she says. Join. Join. Join what? Join whatever group she is in this week, a group that you are sure to agree with but have no interest in joining. I'm not a joiner, I say. I'm an artist, I say, thinking that somehow makes it worthier. So what? she says.

*I*t worries me, she wrote—she is living in Seattle now— my capacity for hating men. I try so hard to believe in them and then I get a setback. My friend, she came out here and stayed with me for a couple of weeks. She moved to Colorado to be with her boyfriend. One month later, he took all of the money out of their savings account and drove off in their car. He left her a note. He said he didn't like her making more money than him and he didn't see why she had to go to school at night too. Do you think it is impossible, she wrote me, for a woman to be independent and in a relationship too? It worries me. By the way, how are you?

*H*ere, he says, softly. Here, he reaches across the table and lets a pair of earrings slide gently from his palm to mine. Here, he says, softly and so sweetly, intimately, you left these behind last night. Here. Yes, here. Not sadly, because of the way the left side of his mouth curls up smiling a secret sweet lover's smile. Here. Yes, here.

*T*here were two kids. That meant that they had done It twice, whatever It was. Something to do with rubbing stomachs. Maybe bellybuttons.

One morning they came out of their bedroom in a particularly good mood, all smiles and touches. And Daddy's pajamas weren't snapped right. Lizabeth whispered to me that we were gonna have another baby. She was two years older, she knew these things. Mommy's gonna get fat and then we'll have a baby, she said. Something to do with bellybuttons.

I watched and I waited. The next day. And the next. But she didn't get any fatter and we never did get another baby. They must not have done It, Lizabeth said.

*H*e was telling me about his last lover, about what had gone wrong. She was young, he says, she had things to do. An image of a nubile, soft-skinned girl comes to mind, a pretty girl with things to do. She didn't have time to make a commitment, he says. She only wanted to see me occasionally. When she told me that, I went out and got drunk. In the middle of the day. It was the only time I've ever gone out and gotten drunk by myself, he says.

*I*t was Friday night and we lay watching a late-night movie on television—a forties version of Cleopatra. She sat on her throne, imperiously handing a chalice to a long parade of men. Each drank apprehensively, some only under the guards' duress, and went aside to die. Some writhed in pain, some collapsed instantly. Cleopatra remained unmoved, cooly going about her business. A stranger entered the room and questioned one of the guards about the odd doings.

The queen is testing poisons, he was told.

Cleopatra continued until she ran out of men.

Clean up this mess at once, she ordered as she exited.

*G*ary has this certain grin that breaks across his face after making love. Pleased with himself, proud even, like a little boy who just stole a candy bar and got away with it. And sometimes he says this, he says, My, my, my.

*H*e's just someone I'm seeing. Nothing to get alarmed about. He's just someone I go out with. Don't start planning a future for us. Please don't start that.

*T*he Black Hole. That's what they call it. The Black Hole. Just a nickel-and-dime operation, nothing hard. The cops let it slide.

We walk in through the windowless spray-painted door. No need to knock or buzz. If they don't like you, you'll know about it soon enough. The floor, the ceiling, the walls, all are painted black, depthless black. On the far wall, there's a panel with a one-way sliding mirror. He speaks into it. Just a nickel bag today, Hal says as he slides a five-dollar bill through. A tiny plastic bag of grass appears. Hal sticks it in his back pocket. We hold the door open for entering people as we leave.

It's not that great a deal, Hal says when we're back out on the street, our eyes adjusting to the light, but it is convenient.

I sleep with the lights on now. I don't really sleep much. I listen. Listen to the mice play football in my bedroom. Every few minutes, I throw books in their direction, hoping to intimidate them. I have put pink granular poison in little trays called Ratkups in the corners. It causes internal bleeding. Soon, I will hear them drag their invalid feet across the floor. And then I will hear nothing, only smell their rotting bodies. Why are you so cranky? Larry asks. Don't tell me you have insomnia again.

*H*e loves baseball. He loves the Yankees. How could you not? he asks. He tells me about specific players, about incidents and personalities and managers and games. Those Yankees. Come to a game with me, he says, and then you'll see.

We buy a fifth of Jack Daniels and a program. I try to be enthusiastic. Or at least pay attention. He is enthusiastic. Very. Three rows ahead of us sits a gaunt young man in an overcoat, its ragged collar pulled high up on his neck. He holds a transistor radio tight to his ear, as if he would push it in if he could. He rocks back and forth, smiling, grimacing. He's blind.

I edge closer to Gary and reach for the whiskey. He's depressed. The Yankees are losing. To the Red Sox no less. Those Yankees.

*N*o middle-of-the-night phone calls from this boy. No predawn panics. What makes sense in daylight makes sense at night and vice versa and that's the way it should be, right? No histrionics, please, we are adults now, we have learned to be polite. We have learned order and logic and manners. We have learned not to be adolescents.

No insomnia for this boy. A hard day's work, a good night's sleep. Problems can't be solved in the dark, there's no sense in thinking about them, right? Be reasonable, make sense, make sense.

Please do not disturb. It is written on his face. Not a hardened face, not a scarred one, it can even be a kind face, but please do not disturb, especially after business hours. There is a time and a place for everything. He learned that early, he believes that now. It makes sense, after all. Even I know that. Transactions made in the dark are nullified by light. Go about your business, go on, go on. Disruptive conduct is not appreciated here. It's not even understood.

*C*arrie's apartment is filled with lilies. Lots and lots of lilies and other white flowers I don't know the names of. All pale and sweet. She has become friendly with the funeral director who works next door. He doesn't see the point in letting all those flowers go to waste, and neither does she.

Mark thinks it's morbid, she says, but I think he's just jealous. Though I wouldn't mind if they had a little more color.

*M*y first life-drawing class. Eight in the morning for three hours. Thirty-second sketches, three-minute sketches, three-hour sketches. Follow instructions, follow the lines.

For the first half of the semester, we had a female model. She came into the studio in a robe, took it off, assumed whatever pose she was instructed to assume, and held it for however long she was instructed to hold it for. We drew. She was what you would call curvaceous with long blond hair. She was a good model.

For the second half of the semester, we had a male model. He came into the studio in a robe, took it off, assumed whatever pose he was instructed to assume, and held it for however long he was instructed to hold it. He too was a good model. He wore a jock strap. Really.

*B*asic sex. Good because it is tender, good basic sex. No frills attached. Nothing ornate. Nothing baroque. This is what we do. Yes? Yes, of course, I suppose it is. I suppose so. No, no, I don't want just the attachments without the body, no I don't want merely the fringe benefits, no, I don't, but . . . But what?

I can show you something. You wanna see? Or aren't I supposed to know those things. Where on earth did you learn that? I don't know. Nowhere. I just know it. Maybe I shouldn't say anything. Maybe I shouldn't show anything. I don't know any better, you know? Or any different.

But I do, I do. See, look here, if you do this, I will like it, you see? I can show you. Do you see? I want you to see. I want to see. Isn't there something you are leaving out? Yes, yes, it is hip sex, of course it is. I go here, you go there, that's how it's done these days. You know that. You obviously know that. But there can be more. You wanna see?

*T*his week's hit song is replaced by next week's. Dinner parties replace clubs. Nothing seems to replace the humidity. My flower boxes blossom and make me happy. My painting progresses—but I think laterally. Time for new subject matter.

A dream. I am pregnant. Very pregnant. I am in a hospital, about to give birth. I have a husband. He is there. He is faceless, though, I don't know who he is. And there are others there too. There is someone, someone I know, but I don't know who, who is going to videotape the event. He says, Okay, ready. And I am supposed to be ready. But I'm not. I'm not in labor, I say. But the tape is ready, he exclaims. I grunt and groan, trying to induce labor. But I can't. I'm not in labor, I repeat. But the tape is ready, he repeats, frustrated.

*S*ince when did taking a picture of your lover in stilettos rate a gallery? Really.

*H*ow does it look? she asks.

Horrible, I say. Part of it is red, part of it is purple. What do I do?

C'mon, Carrie says, it's probably not as bad as you think.

It is, I reassure her, this time I really blew it.

You'll get used to it.

I don't want to get used to it. How are you?

I'm okay, she says.

You sure don't sound it, I say. Carrie doesn't usually call at three in the morning, even if she is curious about my hair.

I don't know, she says.

What is it?

Sara?

Yes?

I need direction.

I half-laughed. Carrie, everyone needs direction at three in the morning.

No, I mean it. I mean it. I'm twenty-eight fucking years old and I still have no idea what I want to do with my life.

It's summer. You should never try to figure these things out in summer. I didn't know want to say to her. I'm not always so sure either, you know, I add.

Yeah, but at least you have your painting.

How simple she made it sound. It wasn't that simple. Or was it?

It's not going so well, I say. There are times when I want to forget about painting completely. I'm tired of always being broke.

We should think of a business to go in to.

What?

I don't know. Anything.

Okay, I say. And I thought okay too. In the meantime, though, I say, You don't know of anything that removes henna, do you?

No. Listen, I'll see you tomorrow and maybe we can come up with something.

Okay.

Goodnight.

Goodnight.

*J*effrey is driving a cab now and he says there's nothing like it to teach you about neurosis. Better than a doctorate, he says. He says as soon as someone opens their mouth, he knows exactly what their problem is. He says he never wants to make small talk again.

*T*hey lived together for five years. They both went to medical school. They got married. Everyone said, Finally. It's about time. Three months later, they decided on an amicable divorce. They live in California. I don't know all the details. Only that.

*I*t was all going to be perfect. This little dinner. Gary. Mark and Carrie. I spent the whole goddam day working on it and it was only soup and salad. But I really did want everything to be perfect. Special. A special evening. And it was going fine, too. Perfect. Until the buzzer rang and I made the mistake of letting him in.

I didn't realize you'd have company, he said, as if we had just seen each other yesterday and had made some sort of plans. What do you want? I asked. Curt. I was surprised to see him, of course, but not really. It was crucial that the rest realize that he was more than unexpected, that he was unwanted. This, of course, amused him. I just wanted to see you, he said, aren't you going to offer me some wine? He reached to kiss my cheek. He was high, very high. I stepped back. What do you want? I asked again. I miss you, he said. He scanned the room. What a bonus to have an audience. He was clearly enjoying himself. Get out of here, Brett, I said. I was not going to yell. Aw, c'mon, Sugar, aren't you glad to see me? Haven't you missed me? Just a little? Don't you remember how good it was with us? His voice was mocking, sure of himself. Get out of here, I said. I love you, he said, give me one more chance. You don't know how, I said. Well then, teach me, he said, teasing, teasing. I think. Get out of here, I yelled. Aw, c'mon, there's nothing wrong with us seeing each other every now and then, is there? I knew there was, I couldn't right then remember exactly what, but I knew there was. Can't you understand, I screamed. There was only us in the room now, no Carrie or Mark or Gary, just us. I don't want to see you. I don't want your kind of love. I am not going to clean up after you. Don't you understand that? Go find yourself someone else to wash your face. Just get out of here. Get out of here. I stopped. Self-conscious. There were, after all, other people in the room. Cunt, he said. You cunt. And he left. I went back to the table. Bastard. Junkie bastard.

*H*oney, coursing through my veins, rattling my arms and womb. Honey, tingling my cheeks, stuck in my throat, wrapping around the tip of my tongue.

Honey, honey, how I long for someone to call Honey, a man, a child, honey, honey, just want someone to call Honey.

*W*hy won't you talk to me?

I said it to him. He says it to me. Why won't you tell me what's going on. I said it to him. Now someone is saying it to me. Why won't you talk to me? The silence, this time, is mine. And it's not less painful than the asking. I had thought it might be, but it isn't.

I never thought I'd be unable to tell you what's going on. I never thought I'd be so bottled up. There is so much I could tell you, if only I could. And I want to, understand that, please understand that. I want to. I don't know what's stopping me. I flush with the words. I wish I could draw it for you. Since I seem to have so much trouble saying it. Saying anything. There's so much I could draw for you. But you need words. I understand that. I did too. I still do. Believe me, I still do. Your words. My words. I need that too. Have patience. Please, have patience. They will come. Just have patience. Please.

*H*e's so young, too young. A street waif with a rich father and a sadistic boyfriend and a charming way about him. Frustrating too, at times. When he acts like a little queen, when he cruises a Hell's Angel, when he whines about the color of my carpet.

Romantic boy, with a pocket full of keys, but no home, scrounging money for food or drugs, thinking you finally belong to a tradition, a great lower east side beat tradition. Stupid boy, don't you know it's easy to be broke? Silly boy, you fucked over your best friend and made off with his lover. You'll get yours. A *jeune artiste,* you give up your painting for any old piece of ass. And now you say you're looking for security? Good luck, baby.

You want me to take care of your plants while you're out looking. You want me to clean up your face, all scratched up after your latest spat. You want advice. You want my lights to be on when you need to talk. You want five bucks. Sure, kid.

But listen, there's something you should know. I can't make sense of it all for you. And I can't believe your illusions with you. And I most certainly don't have any leftover stability to offer you. And another thing. I have lost patience with your new revolutions and your new societies. But of course, you are young, after all.

I was about ten or eleven. My father took me to the Guggenheim Museum. As we stood before one of Kandinsky's later canvases, he said, Abstract art is just a pimple on the face of the history of art. I didn't say anything. Years later, it came back to me as I was looking in the mirror, and I thought how a single pimple can affect one's entire psyche.

*F*rank, the bartender, went to Las Vegas for the week with his Bartenders' Club. They pay dues each week and then they go to Vegas once a year for a good time. Frank did not have a particularly good time this year. The rooms were too expensive, he said, and so were the girls. And he lost at the tables too.

I used to be a very serious artist, he said. In my formative years. You know, eighteen to twenty-five.

What happened? I asked.

I took acid.

And that was that?

Well then, he said, I realized the whole trip, as we used to say, for what it was. And I gave it up. Now I buy a little pot and a few pieces of coral when I have the money. He lifted the necklace that hung on his neck. This one is Tibetan, he said.

I admired it.

*S*he is close to six feet tall. She is thirty. She is a singer, cabaret-style. She has gigs now and then in little-known clubs and restaurants. She is from Minnesota.

At seventeen, she ran away to Canada. She slept in churches, she was deported, she returned. She worked for the phone company. She waitressed. Once, when she was particularly desperate, she took a job picking worms. They take you to a field, she says, and strap a bucket of sawdust on your left leg, worms are slippery, and an empty bucket for the worms on your right leg. They pay you nine dollars per thousand worms. I made seven dollars.

She moved back to New York.

*M*y father takes the matches out of my hands and lights my cigarette, despite the fact that he doesn't approve of my smoking. Another martini? he asks.

That would be nice, I say.

You know, Sara, he says, I have never cared in the least what you do, so long as you are self-sufficient.

I know.

And it appears you are. Self-sufficient, that is.

Yes.

But I must say, I am just a bit curious. What exactly are your plans?

Plans?

Well, you must think about your future, he says, handing me the drink. It seems to me that if you must continue with your painting, you should find someone who is able to take care of you.

Take care of me?

You know, a husband. It does make sense, he says. Am I right?

Of course, I say.

And that is that and we are both relieved, for he has taken care of his paternal duties for the next year or two and now we can sip our martinis and talk about the President and real estate as usual.

I looked at my crinkled, pruny fingers. It will go away, I reassure myself, they will turn normal again. When I was young, I used to be afraid that a snake would wriggle out of the faucet as I soaked in the tub. It would come slithering out and wrap around me and . . .

I was remembering this as I watched Gary's big toe stop up the faucet opening. What protection he gave unknowingly. I took another hit off the joint and reached over to bring it to his mouth, futilely trying to keep it dry. We laughed, we let the cinders fall, we embraced. Slipping, sliding, colliding against the tile boundaries, we came, we came up for air, we came out bruised.

His big toe had long since left the faucet, and still, no serpent.

I cannot deal in probabilities. It would paralyze me. I can say, Yes, it is possible, or no, it is not. But not probable or improbable. That would only immobilize me.

My painting is possible. I know that. Yes, I know that. I don't know if it is probable. You use that to measure success. That is how you do it. That I can't answer for you. That is not the question. Not mine, anyway. You are welcome to it. That's your business. That is the language of dealers. I am not a dealer. Not yet. That is the language of insomnia. It is morning now. It is not the issue.

It is possible. I know that. It is morning and it is possible. That's all that matters. For now, anyway.

*S*he is fat. Massively, blubberingly, rolling and rippling fat. She has thick chestnut hair and enormous eyes that are always scrupulously made up. She has a beauty mark on her right cheek. She looks like an opera singer. But she isn't. She's an actress. She used to teach Spanish to junior high-school kids. She used to be married. Now she takes classes. Now she is single.

Did I ever tell you about my parents? she asks. Did I ever tell you that they are millionaires? She is explaining how she is getting the money to go to a ritzy fat farm next week. She enunciates each word as if making sure it would reach the last row of a large theater.

Every year, on the night of the Academy Awards, she puts on an evening gown and drinks champagne as she watches the festivities on television. It is my favorite night of the year, she says, my absolute favorite.

I am good. I swear to fucking god. I am good.

*H*e sits in his room by candlelight. Even in the morning. Sometimes he smokes a pipe. Sometimes he burns incense, the cheap conical kind. Usually, he just stares at the candle. He has boxes of them. He buys them wholesale.

He reads *Penthouse* and *Hustler*. He saves the back issues, keeping them in careful chronological order. He doesn't like other people to look at them. He loves his grandmother. He talks about her constantly. She is the ideal woman. He used to talk to a psychiatrist. He doesn't anymore. It's too much effort, he says. Almost everything is too much effort, he says. He never raises his voice. He is polite, god is he polite. Often he sits in a room with other people and doesn't say a word for hours. He doesn't want to interrupt. He chuckles to himself.

One day, David says politely, one day, I am either going to kill someone else or kill myself. And then he goes back to his room.

*G*oing out on a date—can you believe it? a date—even though he's the only man I've been seeing, this was a date, and putting in my diaphragm before I go out because timing isn't all that important right then, and I just take it for granted that we will end up spending the night together and it will make things easier, and then coming home alone.

It started out okay, nice even, and then, well, we were in this club and it was so crowded and I kept running into people that I knew. It's not that I wanted to see them, but what could I do? I smiled and breezed through it and he stood off in a corner and looked absently around him and I could tell he wasn't having much fun at all, and I said, Tell me when you want to go, okay? but he said, No, everything is alright, and he stepped back disgruntled and silent and robotic while I kissed cheeks and no one was having any fun, just trying real hard, and then he says he isn't feeling well and has to go home, but I should stay cause I'm having such a good time, and he leaves.

I stayed another fifteen minutes or so and I didn't talk to anyone else except to tell a few teen-age boys to get lost and I wasn't having a good time to begin with, I was sick to death of it all, the masquerade crowds and the rock'n'roll noise, and I didn't want to be there, not back there, no, I would rather have been in a quiet place talking to him, we shouldn't have gone there to begin with and I certainly didn't want to be there alone.

So I left too and bought the Sunday paper and leafed through the magazine section until I was too tired not to sleep and I left my diaphragm in cause it would have been too goddam sad to pull it out that night.

*I*t all dissolves. It all completely dissolves. There is no time or thought, there is only the painting, the canvas, the brush. The only structure is internal, the only geometry is the one that I transmit from mind to canvas, there is nothing else. There are no thoughts of the night before or the next day, there is no later, there is nothing, it all dissolves. There is only me, only the unique relationship between the paper and my eye, the triangle that excludes all else, the magical triangle that dissolves all else.

*H*e called for no particular reason, none that I could figure out, anyway, and we talked about the ballet he had just seen and he played his calculator for me, it plays a selection of tunes, and then he said he was going to bake chocolate chip cookies and he said goodbye.

*S*he is a painter too. She says, Whenever I am in love, I paint myself into the canvas. When I'm not in love, I don't. I tell her that I have been working on self-portraits again lately, so this is not an issue.

*J*ohn the Baptist just whizzed by on roller skates. Really.

*J*ohn's thinking of joining the Merchant Marines. Why are you laughing? he asks. I'm serious. I could cook, right, I could cook out there. It seems as good a way as any of drying out. I'm going to look into this. It would do me good if I didn't see this place for a while. Besides, the limo company fired me. This would be perfect, he says, see the world and that whole bit. Sure, why not? I think I'm going to join the Merchant Marines. You see if I don't.

*L*arry's latest purchase—a cat, seal point Siamese, nine weeks old, male, named Elvis. Elvis is having trouble getting accustomed to the kitty litter. Actually, it is Larry who is having the trouble. Elvis is quite content, after all, to piss on the floor, preferably under the bed.

What about Pampers? I suggest.

I really think it is too early for Elvis to be making a fashion statement, Larry says, don't you?

*L*izabeth went to an all-girls college. One of the Seven Sisters, actually. Why don't you come here, she said, when I was thinking what college I might like to go to.

I went to visit her. The campus was all castles and lakes and green beauty and pretty girls in white tennis dresses laughing. Lizabeth took me to the library and the new arts center, which was big and angular and shiny. See? she said, you would love it here.

At night, we drank beer with her roommate from Virginia and talked about boys and mixers and diamond engagement rings. I had an interview the next day and I got an application and I had tea with a few of the professors and then I went home.

I don't think it's for me, I told my parents. Well, it's good enough for your sister, they said.

*H*e wants to know everything. Faces. Names. Dates. What happened. Where. And why. Why. I want to know, he says, so I can understand. And so I tell him. One night, I tell him everything he wants to know. And then some. I give him so many details. Details I thought I had forgotten. Details I never told anyone. Details that are best left locked in the vaults of personal memory.

I'm tired, he says. I've got to get up early in the morning. It's time I le——. . . . Okay, I say. I didn't need to hear the rest. He laughs. Why are you laughing? I ask. You didn't have to say okay so quickly, he says.

*W*hy have you never asked what kind of birth control I use?

I just assumed you were on the pill.

Why would you assume that?

Isn't everyone?

No, everyone isn't.

You mean you're not?

No, I'm not.

Oh.

Yes. Oh.

What do you use then?

A diaphragm.

You're kidding.

No, I'm not kidding.

Why in god's name didn't you ever tell me?

Why in god's name didn't you ever ask?

*H*e tells me he has an impulsive, an impetuous, side. He tells me of things he has done, things that make no sense. And I'm supposed to take his word for it. I can be irrational, he says.

And yet, all I see is the discipline, the manners. If there is recklessness, it is buried deep below the gravity level of protocol. I would like to hit that nerve. I would like to witness that wildness. Then maybe I would believe him, believe us.

*S*andra has just come from her ex-husband's opening. It was my work, she says.

Sandra was married to Tom for ten years. He taught art history at a university upstate. She was a university wife. She did her painting. When things were good, she says, he would ride me on the back of his bicycle singing opera. Then he fell in love with one of his students. She threw dishes out the window when he rode up on his bicycle.

Since the divorce, they have both moved to New York. He has remarried. She has not. They are both painting. That bastard ripped off my work, Sandra says, and I'm not just saying that cause his new wife was standing there gloating.

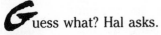

*G*uess what? Hal asks.

What?

It's been, let's see, thirty-six and twelve, it's been almost fifty hours since I smoked.

Cigarettes? I ask, somewhat amazed. Hal does like his Camels.

No, grass. I haven't had a joint in almost three days.

That's great.

I want you to know, he says, feeling that I am not sufficiently impressed, that I have not gone that long without getting high since 1974.

That's great. What's the occasion?

Well, it's just taking me too long to get this painting done.

I figure I'll be able to work faster if I don't have to marvel over every detail for five hours.

Good luck.

Yeah.

*T*here is something missing. But it's okay. Maybe it's what's missing that makes it okay. I don't tingle. And I don't cry. Nothing cuts. Nothing stings. It's okay.

But there are times when I resent him. Resent him for not inciting the passion within that I'm missing. I can take it in stride. There is no reason to run. In either direction.

Only sometimes, I wish there were.

I hear he's touring now, he and the band.

There's always someone walking around who wants to tell me what he's doing. They say he's touring now.

*H*e has these friends, Bob and Rennie, they are quite nice, I don't know them real well, but they seem quite nice. Bob and Rennie invited us over for drinks. One couple invites another couple over for drinks, right? I had already made plans to go over to Larry's to see what he was working on, so I said, Yes, I would love to come, but I would have to meet Gary over there. About ten.

Larry and I sat on stools around his work table and talked about different weights of paper and the growing expense and we drank cheap vodka out of paper cups and we talked more and we drank more and he said, Look, I have some opium. Do you want to smoke some? And I said, I don't think so, I have to make it uptown by ten to meet Gary, but I must not have sounded very convincing because he said, C'mon, you've got plenty of time, and he was right, I did, and besides, I was enjoying myself and I figured, why not, why not enjoy myself more? Things were good and I liked talking the mechanics of art with Larry, the specifics of one artist to another, and Gary would be there and everything was fine. Sure, why not? I said. So we smoked some and drank some more and played with his new box of crayons and then the phone rang. It's for you, Larry said, after saying Yeah into the receiver twice. What the hell are you still doing there? Gary's voice boomed, really boomed, into the receiver, into my ear and through my head. It's eleven o'clock. We were getting worried. Did you forget? No, I didn't forget. I was laughing. I was aware that I was laughing and that I shouldn't be laughing but I kept on laughing nevertheless and Larry was laughing too. I'm glad you find it amusing, Gary said. He was hurt. He had a right to be. I knew that. I'm on my way, I said, as contritely as possible. It doesn't sound to me like you're in any shape to be on your way anywhere, he said. No, I said, I'm fine. Actually, I'm wonderful, absolutely wonderful. I'll be there in a few minutes. So what if my words were slurred and far, far away. At least I wasn't laughing anymore. Don't bother, he said. Look, I said, I just lost track of time. It's nothing to get all upset about. I'll be there. His anger seemed absurd to me. Don't bother, he said again and hung up.

He's very angry with me, I said to Larry. Oh no, he said, laughing childishly. Oh yes, I said, laughing childishly. And

I'm very upset about it, I said, laughing more, very upset. Well then, he said, we'll just have to smoke some more, won't we? Absolutely, I said. The cloying sweet heavy smell of opium filled the studio. Later, hours, maybe, I don't know, Larry walked me to a cab, pipe in hand, and gave the driver directions to my apartment. I slept in the back until the driver said, We're here, miss, and then I paid him and got out and found my keys and went inside and I thought, I'm sorry, I'm sorry, I never do things like this, I'm sorry Gary, I just lost track of time, I'm sorry, and I fell asleep with all my clothes on.

*W*atching Sesame Street with a six-aspirin hangover headache and a static buzz that you had never noticed before now searing into your brain and down your spine and thinking about five-year-olds with skin so fine it hurts, it hurts to think of them and to think of yourself, but you're too goddam hungover to cry about it and why don't you just turn the fucking thing off? Cause there's nothing else, now is there, just what in hell are you supposed to do with a head too gripped to sleep?

*H*al gives me the plates to serve. Vegetable for him. Swiss for her. Shaved carrot sticks stand up perpendicular to the fluffed-up eggs, and deep red peppers lie flat across. Sliced strawberries circle one, blueberries, the other. The couple looks up to me for an explanation.

The cook is into Russian Constructivist omelettes this week, I say.

*P*hil Donahue likes being concerned. He likes ripping off his glasses and giving the camera a close-up of his concerned face. He likes having concerned shows and he certainly always has a concerned audience. He is definitely a concerned man. It's an alright thing to watch at nine in the morning.

Last week, he had on a medical team who think they've found a new spot in women deep in their vaginas that can give them pleasure.

Have you looked for it, darling? Errol asks. He saw the show too. Have you had someone look for it? No? Well, I must tell you, darling, I have found it in one of my dogs.

*T*he three of us. Sitting on his couch.

Her hands like a young/old woman's, white white skin so skinny, that big pulsing vein standing up like the Verrazano bridge and the knuckles like gradated skulls.

His hands, man's hands, thick and slightly discolored, broad, short nails, calloused hands resting on his knees. I would like them on me, slowly, calmly. I would like his man's hands on me.

So. Take away your hands. So that I might have his. On me.

*L*et's go dancing, I say. Okay, he says. And that night, we go dancing. Swing dancing. Sweaty sexy fun dancing. We smooch between dances. Later, our legs ache from dancing so much.

That wasn't a bad idea, he says.

No, not bad, I think, not bad.

*S*he was ironing her nightgowns. Well, I have to do something, Carrie says. Did I ever tell you about the insurance salesman from Chicago?

No, I say.

Well, it was at the end of my great European adventure and I was broke. I mean flat broke. I was sleeping for the last couple of days in an airport and I didn't even have money for a pack of cigarettes. So this guy started talking to me and he seemed harmless enough and he asked me to go have a drink with him. I told him that I didn't have any money but he said he had plenty. So we went and had a few drinks and then he bought dinner. His flight was the next morning too. He bought me cigarettes. You know what he wanted? All he wanted was to play with my hair. He was happy just sitting there wrapping strands of hair around his fingers. There have been worse deals, Carrie says.

She puts down the iron. You know, Sara, she says, I could really love Mark. It feels, I don't know, it feels real to me. You know what I mean? It never felt real with anyone before. It could really work. I mean, I can actually envision the whole bit with him, marriage, kids, the whole shebang. We could have it all. I've never thought that before. But we could have it all. At least we have a chance.

He made me think, she says. He really made me think about what I want and how I act and the difference between the two. You know, she says, I'm really not the wild girl that people seem to think I am. I want some security too, she says.

She starts ironing again. I keep waiting to stop wanting him, she says, but I don't. I just keep on becoming more and more sure. I don't believe it, she says, I really am in love with him. Do you think I should tell him? she asks.

I went to stay at Paul's country house for the weekend. Actually, it's his father's country house. His father is rich. His country house is an estate in the Hamptons. There is a new clay tennis court and a large pool and about twenty lounge chairs. It looks like a hotel.

I am given a bedroom upstairs to sleep in. It is green and white and yellow and ruffly. I fall asleep while Edith Piaf plays on the new vertical turntable downstairs. I have been drinking brandy. I know I won't have to get out of bed to turn the stereo off. The bed is soft as country beds are. I sleep well.

In the morning, there are coffee and bagels and the Sunday New York Times waiting for us on a table by the pool. We take our time.

In the afternoon, we sit on the porch and drink beers. He is feeling a little low, he says. I'm not feeling anything in particular. Sometimes, he is embarrassed by his wealth. He entered his father's business three months after he graduated from college. Sometimes I wonder what it's like to do something else, he says. Sometimes I feel like moving to Colorado and being a waiter for a year.

We drink more beer. Why don't you? I ask. I can't, he

says, I have too much responsibility. You're lucky, he says, you're doing exactly what you want to be doing. I guess so, I say.

*H*al's father liked hunting. Once a year, he would take me, Hal says. It was supposed to be this big father/son deal. The last time we went, I had a perfect shot, only I didn't fire. I couldn't. My father called me a faggot and hit me in the head with the butt of his rifle. Every time he gets mad at me, Hal says, he calls me a faggot. He says all artists are faggots.

*T*here were no specifics I could hand him, no finite sentences. There was nothing concrete to be analyzed, dissected, resolved. There was only a nameless, faceless dissatisfaction that was strangling my ability to respond.

He had been so patient lately. He had tried coaxing, chiding, listening. He had been good. Kind and understanding. But he didn't understand. And his attempts to break through irritated me. His subtlety slid off me, leaving no marks and no pressing need to answer.

It wasn't made of brick, this wall between us, but malleable plastic, that fogged, that cleared, that shifted position. An insidious distortion that I could not penetrate. Even if I had tried.

I walked out into the living room. I would try. But before I got close enough to say anything, he muttered, It's crap.

What? I wasn't sure what was crap.

You and your great artistic pretensions. Pure crap. His face was contorted with anger. He wanted to hurt me, that was clear, he wanted to hurt me badly.

Being an artist is your goddam excuse for everything. You're an artist, so you have to be treated specially because you're so fucking sensitive, you're so fucking superior to everyone else. You have some almighty excuse for living out your two-bit bohemian fantasy, and everyone else can be damned. Well, I'm fed up with it. I don't even think you give a fuck about making art.

He stopped suddenly. It had always been our demilitarized zone—my art. It was not up for questioning.

What the hell do you know? My gut twisted and burned. The only thing you know about art is how to sell toothpaste. If you think I'm so full of crap, why don't you leave and let me get some work done. I don't need you.

I turned my back to him. I waited for him to head for the door.

I'm sorry, he said softly, I didn't mean it. It's not that at all.

I know, I said, knowing too that I would always wonder.

Tell me though, what's happening to us.

I don't know.

I do believe in you, in your work, you must know that.

I think I do.

He reached over and pulled me to him and we stood there in the middle of the room, clinging to each other as those in the presence of an unknown danger have a tendency to do.

*L*isa calls. Hello, she says, this is Lisa.

Oh yes, I say. Hi.

I don't know if Hal told you, she says, but I'm looking for my own space.

Oh.

Do you know of anything?

Not off-hand.

You know, she says, this has nothing to do with anything. We're still together. You're sure you don't know of anything?

No, I say, but I'll let you know if I hear of something.

Thanks, she says.

*P*roof. You all want proof. You all want to be sure. Well, let me tell you, there is nothing in this goddam world I want more than for you to have your proof. And I'm gonna give it to you, I swear I am.

And yeah, I wanna see your faces when you get it. Yes I do. I want to see all of your faces, the pleasant ones saying, Why don't you go into commercial art, dear? and the smug ones saying, Pay her no mind, she's just one more, they're a dime a dozen. Yes, I want to see your faces when I have my first one-woman show, my first piece in a museum, when you have your proof.

What? You mean she was talented after all? Well, why didn't anyone tell us?

*I*t can be fun again. It is fun again. I had forgotten that that was possible, forgotten that that was the way it was supposed to be. But it is. Fun. More fun than anything else.

*A*ren't you going to answer the phone? I ask.

Absolutely not, Carrie says.

But what if it's important?

It's not important, it's only Mark.

The same Mark you were in love with last week?

The same Mark who didn't call me when he was supposed to last night. He'd better get it straight from the start. I am not going through that kind of stuff with him. I mean business.

Besides, Carrie says, boys may be boys, but that doesn't mean we have to encourage them.

*I*t feels good. Drinking vodka and smoking joints and cigarettes. Scanning rock'n'roll stations, scanning the *History of Art,* that fat old book. It feels good.

There's a breeze coming through the window, prancing over me. Summer is ending and it feels good. It feels so very good to be painting again.

I wanna paint, paint, paint. And I wanna be good, real good. I just wanna be good.

*I*t's getting dark earlier now. Tomorrow is September. Thank god, we all say. Enough already, we all say. We get the point.

*A*ll of us who worked there had the same scars. Stripes of browning burn marks on our right forearms. Left, on a few, of course. A faulty oven, poorly placed.

Branded, Hal says, branded for life.

*N*ew York at dawn. Imagine it. We stood on the lumpy tar roof determined to see New York at dawn. It used to be so much easier to stay up all night, Carrie says, have you noticed that? Age, I say, joking, joking of course. We did not feel ourselves to be aging at all. We were young, so young. Young with New York lightening up before us, for us, as if it were a movie set being gradually lit for our benefit alone. New York beneath and around and above us, the granite and glass not yet glistening. Vulnerable, attainable even, our New York, our city.

New York at not quite dawn, the smell neither day or night, but somewhere shifting below, our New York, a paste-up of toy structures to be moved about in the unclaimed hour when everything, yes everything seems possible, how could it not?

We will make it, Carrie says. Yes, we will, I say, and know that it is true, how could it not be? The streets are empty still. Of course we will make it, we will, but later, now it is time for sleep, breakfast perhaps, but sleep, sleep. We are both suddenly too tired to wait for the red pink entry of the day. Well, we almost made it, Carrie says, as we climb down the fire escape.